A Taste of Privilege

Madelene Yahya

Chapbook Press

Schuler Books
2660 28th Street SE
Grand Rapids, MI 49512
(616) 942-7330
www.schulerbooks.com

A Taste of Privilege

ISBN 13: 978195769095

Library of Congress Control Number: 2022907641

Printed in the United States by Chapbook Press.

To my uncle Bob. You inspired me tremendously. Our time together was priceless, and I miss you dearly. The memory of you will live on through me.

Acknowledgments

Most importantly, I would like to thank my Heavenly Father and Jesus Christ my Lord and Savior, whose love showed me that I was capable of writing this book and gave me the determination to see it through.

To my mother and father, Elizabeth and Marzine O'Neal. To my children, Ryan, Alisha, Erica, and Tevana. To my backbone, Dorothy Bennett. To Betsy Garner, Uncle McKinley, and Cousin Elise. Each one of you has encouraged, supported, and loved me in your own unique way. For that, I am beyond grateful.

The year was 1918. Woodrow Wilson was the 28th president of the United States of America, in which he served under the Democratic Party. This was also the year that the United States came under attack from the Spanish flu pandemic. Well over 500 million lost their lives to that horrific disease. The Spanish flu was brought to the United States by the military; it originated on a base in Kansas on March 11, 1918. The state of Mississippi had a death toll of over 6,219 from this deadly disease which killed mostly babies and young adults ages 25-35 throughout the state.

At that time, African Americans were dealing with social problems including racial barriers in medicine. Black people were forced to have their own separate hospitals, as well as their own doctors and scientists to treat the pandemic. They received little help from the government. However, the influenza didn't hit the African American communities as hard as it did the white communities. Thank God for his love and favor at that particular time!

One of President Woodrow Wilson's famous quotes is: "The man who is swimming against the stream knows the strength of it." In the year 1918, young McKinley Newton was just 12 years old. One Sunday morning, McKinley was getting ready for church. His mom, Martha Newton, and his dad, Frank Newton, had adopted McKinley as a newborn baby. Martha was a midwife who was well known for delivering babies in the area of Edwards and Vicksburg, Mississippi. This was a typical Sunday, in which, like always, McKinley's parents found themselves waiting on McKinley to groom himself for church; he took pride in looking his best. Eventually, they made their way to Good Hope Baptist

Church as a family. The church sat on a little hill on a dirt road. It was all white--even the steps were white. There were a lot of different people who attended Good Hope Baptist Church, and they were all making their way into the church to get their praise on.

McKinley had always participated in church. He was a young Junior Deacon in training. Now, at the age of 12, he already had his eye on a young girl. It was customary in this time and era that girls would marry young. After church on this ordinary Sunday, without even consulting his parents, McKinley asked for this young girl who was only six years old. Her name was Minnie Marley. She was beautiful, and her hair was long and thick. Minnie's parents were Walter Marley and Beatrice Draper. They had four boys and one girl. McKinley said to Minnie's father, "Mr. Marley, I want to marry your daughter." Mr. Marley smiled and said, "She has four brothers, and we will see about that. She is just a baby, my baby girl."

Standing back looking on was Minnie, smiling but not really understanding what that boy was talking about. She would just run round with the other children. Minnie's four older brothers were named Johnny, Moody, Selvei, and Othea. They had found out what McKinley had asked their dad and had cornered McKinley by himself outside. Johnny said to McKinley, "You'd better leave our sister alone. Don't make us hurt you."

McKinley's father saw what was going on and said to the young boys, "Leave him alone. Y'all just got out of church. Didn't you learn anything? The boys walked away to get their little sister and make their way back home with their parents, Walter and Beatrice. McKinley was told by his dad, "Me and you will have a long talk tonight before you go to bed."

McKinley got in the truck with his parents and they drove back home for dinner. Miz Martha went in the house and got herself undressed from church. Miz Martha set the table with the food that she had already prepared: fried chicken, homemade biscuits, mashed potatoes, and snap green beans. Everyone now sat down to eat together. The Black family in the early 1900's as a unit was strong, with the presence of both parents. Frank Newton began to pray over the food, thanking God for his grace and mercy. When he was finished praying, everyone said, "Amen."   Frank said to his son, "Now, do you want to tell me about what happened today at church?

McKinley said, "Well, Dad, there's this girl that I want to marry, and I know that she is too young right now. I will marry her when she is old enough was all that I asked. I just don't want anyone else to ask for her hand in marriage was all I was asking Mr. Walter Marley when he got all bent out of shape and called her brothers on me. Dad, you know I could have taken them on!

"Now, son," Mr. Newton said, "you know I have taught you to let God fight your battles."

Miz Martha said to her son, "You're too young to be thinking about marriage. You have to finish school. Your education is what is important to me at this time.   McKinley answered, "Yes, Mom, you are right."

They enjoyed their meal and also had good conversation. McKinley asked his parents about his birth mom. Miz Martha said to her son, "Well, sweetie, I know one thing about her. She was very educated. Her name was Loula Hood and she attended Alcorn University where she fell in love with a professor. Yes, he is your father! He is still living, but I just don't know where he is right now. If it's God's will, you, will meet him. You don't even have to worry about that."

McKinley said to both of his parents, "I love you. God gave me to two of the best parents on this earth." Now that made Martha and Frank Newton happy.

Later on that night, Frank and Martha were in their bed when they had a conversation about McKinley, and how, yes, they considered the fact that his father was still living. His name was Henry Nixon. Should they try to find him and see if he wanted a relationship with his son? Martha looked at her husband and said to him, "I am not willing to hurt our son. I think that his father has had all the time in the world to have a relationship with his son. I'm not going to try to help McKinley find his birth father. I just want to focus on making sure he gets the best education that he can get. Making sure that he has God in his life. Frank and Martha went fast to sleep after they had this conversation.

The next morning it was bright and early. You could hear the rooster saying to the world, "Cock-a-doodle-doo!" The birds chirping. You could smell the fresh morning air. See the sun coming up out of the east. McKinley would go outside and gather up the eggs for breakfast. In the smokehouse, that is where the meat was kept. McKinley loved some bacon. His mom would always make sure to serve some along with his meal so he would be full. Everyone waiting and having breakfast.

Then it was time for school. Most of the time McKinley's father would give him a ride to school, and sometimes McKinley would just walk. On this particular day, McKinley was on his way to school, walking and minding his own business. Walking on a gravel road paved with rock, the sky was oh so bright, the weather was a little hot--just an everyday thing in the South. McKinley was walking with a rope tied around his books, which made them easier to carry. McKinley loved singing his church songs that he had learned from church and while attending Sunday School.

Walking in and out of the sun beaming on him, almost halfway to school, as the roads from different directions met up, McKinley could see the other kids walking to school. The Marley boys were walking to school with their little sister, Minnie. At

4

this point everyone walked together. Trying to get to school by 9:00 AM. The name of the school was Sugar Stir Elementary School, which was next door to the church were most of the people in the town attended.

Now everyone was outside in the school yard. All of the children played in the school yard until it was time for the bell to ring, and then everyone would line up to go inside. Everyone heard the bell now, and as they were getting ready to go to their classrooms, McKinley saw Minnie Marley. McKinley said hi to her, and he also smiled at her. Minnie looked at McKinley and she stuck her tongue out at him. Then she said, "I'm not to talk to you. I'm going to tell my brothers on you." McKinley said, "I only said hi to you, and besides, I'm not afraid of your brothers. I can take each of them one on one. I really don't want to get into it, with fighting anyone."

McKinley walked away to make it to his class. He walked very slow-footed, a confident young man with his chest poked out. He had on denim overalls and hard black working boots. He didn't have very many shoes. He wore the same shoes to work in the field with his father Frank. Now in the school, there were about eight classrooms. McKinley was in the room with two of Minnie's brothers, Johnny and Moody. Othea and Selvie were in another classroom. Minnie being younger was also in another group, with the younger children.

McKinley's teacher's name was Mrs. Hanes who, by the way, was a sweet and caring teacher. Mrs. Hanes also taught Sunday School at Good Hope Baptist Church. Mrs. Hanes was writing math problems on the chalkboard when she could hear some talking among the kids in the classroom. Mrs. Hanes had zoomed in on the conversation between McKinley and Johnny. The discussion was about McKinley's feelings for Johnny's little sister, Minnie. Johnny had told McKinley that he'd better stop looking at his sister. McKinley told Johnny, "You can't tell me anything."

Mrs. Hanes had heard the conversation, and she had kindly interrupted, telling both of them that enough was enough. She told both young men that no one wanted to hear their conversation and also expressed to them, "If this continues, I will have some after-school chores for the both of you." Then Mrs. Hanes had gone on with teaching her classroom.

Now it was time for lunch, and then recess. The entire school was playing in the school yard. McKinley was playing with some other kids around his age, tossing the ball around, minding his own business. The Marley brothers were close by. Johnny Marley was playing, and when the ball was tossed to McKinley, Johnny had to jump in the path of the ball to make McKinley miss. Johnny says to McKinley, "You're not that tough, you can't even catch a ball. McKinley stepped back, saying to Johnny, "I'm not going to get in any trouble messing with you. I will see you later. Yes, like after school."

Johnny could see that McKinley had a little backbone in him. Johnny says to McKinley, "Yes, we will."

McKinley says to Johnny, "I'm only one person, and make sure that this is a one-on-one fight." McKinley smiled at everyone. Then he walked away, back to his classroom. Shortly after this incident, the bell rang. All of the teachers were gathering up their children to finish up the day.

A few hours had gone by. It was time for everyone to gather up their things. Now, waiting on the bell to ring, Mrs. Hanes said to her classroom, "Everyone, listen up, I want everyone to take their book home. We have homework. I will be looking for your papers tomorrow. I don't want to hear any excuses." McKinley gathered up all of his things. Now the bell rang. Mrs. Hanes said, "Class is dismissed. I will see you all in the morning."

Now Johnny was outside waiting on his little sister and his three brothers.   Johnny always looked out for them. McKinley didn't have to wait for anyone. He felt as if he needed to resolve what was going on with Johnny Marley now on their walk home, McKinley not wanting any commotion at the school yard. As Johnny and his siblings got farther away from the school yard, McKinley was still close by Johnny, and now the confusion started.   Johnny, tell McKinley! Now talk your stuff now.

McKinley said to Johnny, "You know, let's just get this over with." So, McKinley turned and punched Johnny in his face. Then Johnny punched McKinley.   Then both of them pushed each other.

The other kids were watching and yelling, "Hit him back!" McKinley held his own, the both of them now still calling each other names. The crowd was also moving along the path on their way home. They would fight a while and then walk close on their way home. This was the path that all of the children would walk home every day. The moment was very intense, and now both Johnny and McKinley were on the ground tussling.

The crowd of kids was excited. Oh, it was also very loud! Then, out of nowhere, this little voice calls out, "Look! Look!" It was Johnny's little sister, Minnie.   Her voice got louder.

Johnny and McKinley stopped fighting, and both stood there in shock and fear. Now everyone was looking and yelling out, "Ugh! Ah!" in disbelief at first, as they saw a person's feet--it was a Negro man hanging from a tree! His body was lifeless and looked all beaten up. You could smell the foul odor that came from the body. The birds had started to nibble away at the flesh.

The children stood there for a moment, and then they all held hands and ran as fast as they could to the closest person's house, which was McKinley's house. All of the children stayed together. Sitting on the porch was Frank Newton, McKinley's dad.

Frank stood up; he could tell something was wrong. All of the children were trying to talk at the same time. Frank yelled out in a very loud voice, "Okay, one person at a time."

McKinley said, "Dad! Dad! On our way home was a Black man hanging from a tree." Frank went inside the house to call the police to report what the children had seen on their way home from school. Frank told the other children to go home, their parents would be looking for them.

Now Frank and McKinley got in the truck and went back to the place where the man was hanging from the tree. The police came not too long after they had arrived. There were two officers getting out of the patrol car. Frank and McKinley were standing close to where the man was hanging from the tree. Both of the officers walked toward the body. McKinley was thinking in his mind, yes, these are the good guys, they will make everything, right!

One of the officers said out loud, "I don't know why we came out here, it's just another nigger. Nobody." Frank and his son overheard this. McKinley walked over to his dad because of the way the officer was acting and expressing his own personal feelings about the value of a man, and the fact that this man was Black. Well, McKinley was just taught a lesson when it came to Black men. The officer said to Frank, "Boy! You can call your local funeral home and they can come pick him up, this nigger!" He took his knife and cut the man down, McKinley standing there with disbelief all over his face. He began to sweat; his heart started racing. He felt a lump in his throat; it was hard to swallow this situation. The police got back in their car and drove off.

Frank and his son stood there and watched the officers drive off. Frank had his hand on his son's shoulder. He said, "Son, God be the glory! This is an inhumane act of evil. Son, sometimes being born with brown or dark skin we are looked at as if we are some kind of animal or we are not clean." Frank began to shed a tear.

McKinley said to his dad, "It will get better! Yes, it will get better one day."

"Son, I want you to remember this day! There are some white people that will kill you because of the color of your skin. Son! God says that all men and women are created the same way. Son! I would never tell you to kill a person, or treat them less than yourself, because of the color of their skin. Son! When dealing with the white man, always remember that all white people are not evil. You may have to use your own judgment when you're dealing with white people. Son! Until you know for sure, trust no man and especially no white man. The only one you can trust is God! I'm your dad, son, and I would never lead you down an evil path. I love you, son."

McKinley told his dad, "I love you, too."

"Now, help me put this man in the back of the truck so we can take his body to the funeral home." They picked up the man and put his body in the back of their truck and drove away down the road.

There was as yet no explanation for the Black man found hanging from the tree that particular year. It was later found out that in May of the year 1918, a plantation owner was found murdered. Not knowing who killed him, there was a bounty out for a man called Hazel Hayes Turner. No Black man was safe that year. There were a total of 13 Black men and one Black woman reported hanging from a tree. The woman was pregnant. So, this unborn baby also suffered from the evil of hate.

Later that day, Frank Newton was sitting down at the dinner table with his family, enjoying what his wife had cooked for them. Frank said to his wife, "These last few days have been very trying." Sometimes he would call his wife 'Momma.' He said,

"Momma, I want to thank you for making me this meal." Frank enjoyed the company of his family. Dinner was soon over, and he helped his wife clean off the table.

Troubled by the events of the day, Frank went out into the yard to sit on the back of his truck that was parked close to the house. He had a box that a friend had given him. It needed batteries, so sitting there he put the batteries in this thing call a radio for the first time. It took him a minute. The sound that he heard from the box scared Frank so badly that he dropped it, and lucky it didn't break. Yelling with so much excitement, he called, "Momma!, Momma! McKinley! Come here! Come here! Listen! Listen! There is music coming out of this box! Yes, jazz music." Even though radio had been out since 1895, it was Frank's first time owning one. Frank, his wife and son danced with joy, listening to their new form of entertainment.

So, fascinated with his radio, Frank played around with it. He could hear the news of the day, what was going on in the world. He could even listen to sports like boxing. This was so exciting to Frank. Everyone was talking about the big fight between Jack Dempsey and Barney Lebrowitz (nicknamed Levinsky) in the city of Philadelphia, Pennsylvania. As everyone could see, Frank and his son, McKinley, would be out in the yard listening to the radio for hours until it was night. His wife would have to call the both of them into the house. "It's time for bed, Frank. McKinley, you too. You know you have to get in the house and get your school lesson."

Then both of them would answer, "Yes, Momma, here we come," and Frank would then get himself undressed to get in bed with his wife.

Martha, his wife, said to him, "Sweetie, I'm really glad you enjoy your radio. I'm also glad that you and McKinley have more time with each other, and it's bringing the two of you closer."

Frank told his wife, "Yes, I love my son," as the two of them lay holding each other as they fell fast asleep.

The next morning Frank was out in the yard working on his truck and listening to his radio. He was under the hood of his truck when he heard a vehicle pull up. The door opened. Frank looked up and could see Walter Marley and his boys walking toward him. Walter Marley said, "Good morning!"

Frank replied, "Good morning."

Walter said, "I just wanted to drop by and thank you for making sure that my children were safe and that they made it home the other day."

Frank said, "You're welcome. You know that we have to look out for one another. We have to stick together."

Walter said, "Yes, you're right. We have to be vigilant with one another. You know, I have four young men here, and don't forget about my baby girl! Her name is Minnie." Frank said that she was such a beautiful young lady.

Now just at that time, McKinley walked out of the house. The first person he saw was Minnie. With this goofy look on his face, he said to her, "Hi, Minnie!" As she looked at McKinley, she stuck her tongue out at him and said hi to him. After all of that, McKinley said hi to her brothers Johnny, Moody, Selvie and Othea. Trying not to pay any attention to McKinley's attraction to Minnie, the boys all said hi.

McKinley said to them, "Come look at this baseball card that I have of Babe Ruth."

The boys said, "Yeah, right," with disbelief. Then Johnny said that Babe Ruth was ill with the Spanish flu. Yes, he was gravely ill, but McKinley told the boys that he had heard on his dad's radio that no one really knew for sure whether it was the Spanish flu that had almost taken his life.

The boys all went off to another part of the yard talking as their dads were still standing there trying to start a friendship. Frank was saying, "Come on over anytime, we can drink a little moonshine. Do you drink, Walter?"

"Yes, I drink," he answered with a look of excitement on his face. "Oh, can I bring my wife?'

Frank said, "Sure! That would be wonderful. I believe that our wives know each other from church."

Walter called out to the boys, "Okay, time to get back into the truck. We have things we need to do." Walter told Frank he would talk to him soon. So, from there on out, these two families became very close. They shared Sunday dinners at each other's houses. Martha Newton and Beatrice Draper had gotten so close. They would talk on the phone for hours.

One bright sun-shiny day, Martha asked her husband to take her to the market that was in the next county from where they lived. Frank and his family lived in Warren County, and the market where she wanted to go shopping was in Yazoo County. It wasn't too far from where they lived, about 12 miles away. Frank and Martha talked a great deal on the drive, expressing their feelings about how they were raising their son. They also talked about how God had blessed them with a child. Not quite there yet, Martha started singing "Walk with Me, Lord." Then Frank started to sing, too. Looking at each other, smiling, and holding each other's hand, Frank told his wife, "Momma, I love you!"

She looked at him and said, "I love you too. You are so good to me!"

Frank smiled with this big tear in his eyes. "Momma, you know you make my heart smile." Martha's eyes teared up, too. Frank said, "We are here!" They both got out and walked into the market. There was soap on sale, bags of flour and sugar, other things that Martha needed to keep delivering babies such as peroxide, rubbing alcohol, and some new rags or towels.

Martha looked over and saw a man with a very bright-skinned woman. There was also a little girl with the couple. Martha wasn't sure what she thought she was seeing. The woman and girl looked like white people! So, Martha called out to her husband, "Frank! Frank!" She was close enough to pull him close to her to show him what she was looking at. She whispered in his ear, "I can't believe this. Isn't that Walter Marley over there?" Frank turned to look at this couple talking and laughing. Then, they knew what was going on when Walter leaned over and kissed the woman. Martha's eyes had gotten so big!

With disbelief, Frank said to his wife, "NO! No, it is none of our business!" Yet he still wanted Walter Marley to see him. So, Martha and her husband walked past them, Frank making sure that he spoke to Walter, making sure that Walter saw him. Frank said, "Hey, how are you?"

Walter looked up and was startled by who it was. Then he spoke to Frank, "Hi, how have you been?"

Frank said to Walter,"Oh, I'm really surprised to see you here! Is this your sister?" Walter had an embarrassed look on his face.

Before Walter could answer, the little girl that was with him said with so much excitement in her voice, "Daddy! Daddy! May I please have some rock candy?"

Walter said to her, "Yes, darling, you may." Then to Frank he said, "I need to explain to you. This is my wife," he said as the woman started walking toward them as they were talking. Frank was a bit taken back, yet he said hello to her.

The woman said to Walter, "Where are your manners?" Then she said to Frank, "Hi, my name is Annie Marley! My daughter is also named Annie! My daughter is named after me. They call me Big Annie, and they call my daughter Little Annie!"

Frank was standing there, speechless. Finally, he said, "I'm so pleased to meet you."

She said, "Well, I have never met you before."

Frank said, "Walter and I go back a few months; I guess you can say we are new friends."

"Oh, well, that explains it! It's not too much that I don't know about my husband!"

Frank said, "Well, once again, I'm very pleased to meet you," and then he made his way back to his wife, Martha.

Martha asked, "Well, what was all of that about?"

"I will tell you when we get back in the truck!"

"Ooh, Okay!"

They got in line to pay for their things, and then Frank put everything on the counter. The white man behind the counter said to Frank, "This counter is for white people only." He pointed to the back of the store where a sign over an entrance way said "Colored People Only." Both Frank and Martha were embarrassed. You could see the look of shame on their faces. Frank and Martha gathered up all their things, and as they were making their way to the line for colored people, Frank saw Walter and his other family in the line for White Only. Thinking to himself, Wow, Walter is going for a white man when it is convenient for him. Wow, that Walter Marley is taking advantage of this opportunity. Wow, he has the best of both worlds. When he comes to Warren County, he is a Black man. When he in Yazoo County, he is a white man. Frank was feeling overwhelmed by all of the information he had gathered that morning. He had gotten an earful! Now Frank and Martha got in the truck to go back home. On their way back, Martha asked Frank, "What was all of that about?" Frank explained everything that was said and also what he believed was happening. Martha said to her husband, "Wow, I can't believe what I'm hearing. How does he do that? I'm sure that both of his wives must know about each other. I'm going to tell Beatrice in case she doesn't know! Martha Say!"

"Now, I don't think we should say anything, Momma!" said Frank. "Look at what you're doing and who you would be doing it to. The kids will be the ones mostly affected by this terrible situation. Yes, and they are the innocent ones."

Martha answered her husband, "You're right, sweetheart. Let us find out more about this situation. I'm going to try and talk to Walter when I can." Both of them were saying at the same time that they would pray about it. The rest of the ride was kind of quiet.

When they made it home, pulling up on the side of their house, McKinley was so excited that his parents had made it back from shopping. Running to the truck, he yelled, "Hey, Momma. Hey, Dad! What did you get me?"

His dad said in a very stern voice, "Help us get these groceries in the house and put everything where it needs to go."

McKinley answered, "Yes, Dad!" McKinley told his mom that she had had a few phone calls.

She said, "Yeah, who called?"

"Miz Beatrice and someone from the church."

"You didn't ask who it was?"

"No, I didn't. They said they would call back!"

"Okay, sweetie, just remember next time to please write it down."

"Yes, I will remember."

Frank was in his bedroom taking off his shoes, getting himself more comfortable. He wanted to take his radio outside and enjoy his day. Listening to his music and the news. Frank could also listen to sports like baseball and boxing. This is the way Frank spent most of his day. Or, I should say, his spare time.

Frank also worked as a sharecropper. Yes, back when the slaves were set free, they had nowhere to go, so most of the families would stay on the farm in which their ancestors were once slaves. The owner would let the families tend the fields in exchange for rent to stay on the property. The house that Frank and his family lived in was at the end of the owner's property on a long dirt road. I think they stayed close to the road so families could easily find their way to Miz Martha. She delivered at least one baby a week.

McKinley would help his dad every day tending to the few animals that were on this part of the land. There was a rooster and chickens. There were even two cows. The owner of this property was named Roy Brintal. He would come by the house and talk with Frank, as if they were good friends. Roy would make sure he was able to get anything he could for free, never really doing any work--the eggs that the chickens would lay, the milk from the cows. He even charged Martha for delivering babies! So, if she were paid five dollars, he would want one dollar.

The things Roy would say too; he used the word "nigger" a lot, never biting his tongue. But Frank would ignore him. I guess you could say, until he could do better, he would just keep his peace! McKinley would see his dad take the mental abuse from Roy. He asked his dad one day why he didn't fight back. Frank looked at his son and said to him, "That is why I say to you, get an education. Work hard at whatever you do in life. Learn to save for a rainy day. Trust me, there is always another way to fight your battles. Trust me, son, times will get better. Besides that, me talking to Roy that way--think of the bigger picture. Where would we go as a family? Also, remember when I told you a few weeks ago about trusting no man, also how all white people are not bad. Yet in this case, Roy is someone who is not good. Son, trust in the Lord."

McKinley said, "Yes, Dad! Now let's get in the truck and go to the Yazoo River and see if we can catch us some fish for the fish fry."

So, both of them got in the truck so they could go fishing. Down the road many acres down, there was another landowner who lived on the other side of the property that Roy Brintal owned. His name was Will Montgomery. Mr. Montgomery was known as a very kindhearted man. He was very fair in everything that he would do. In the Black community, when things were wrong, this is the man that would make things right. Frank and McKinley would go out of their way to show their respect for Mr. Montgomery. Riding down the dirt road, they saw him. Rolling down his window, Frank said very loudly, "Good day, Mr. Montgomery."

Answering him, "How are you, Frank? I see your son is growing so fast." McKinley said hello as they waved and made their way to their destination. Now they were sitting on the riverbank with their poles in the water, then they were throwing their lines in the water, never being able to get anything on the pole.

Frank said to his son, "Don't be so easy to give up."

Just as he was saying that, McKinley said, "Dad! Dad!" His eyes had gotten so big with excitement. "I think I got one!"

"Okay, son, calm down and slowly pull your line in. Yes! Nice and slow."

After McKinley had pulled the fish in, he said, "Wow! I love this! Thank you, Dad."

"I didn't do a thing—it was all about you. You did it all on your own. Yes!" After awhile, the both of them had over 40 fish. "I believe that this will be enough for the fish fry."

"Wow, Dad, I want you to know that I had myself a real good time."

"I did too, son." Now, putting their fish in the pail and then in the back of the truck, they made their way back home.

Frank asked his wife to invite some of their neighbors and close friends to come over. He wanted to entertain everyone with his music on his radio. There was also going to be an exhibition fight on the radio and a heavyweight fight, too. Everyone wanted to hear this fight. Yes, it was November 6, 1918, and it was the heavyweight fight between Jack Dempsey and Battling Levinsky. This had been all that Frank had been talking about! He asked his wife, "Could you make some side dishes?" She said yes, she could.

Now it was at the end of the day, and it was getting dark. The music was playing, and you could smell the fish frying. Family and friends started to make their way to the Newtons' house. The yard was full of love. A young man came with one of the neighbors. He had a guitar on his back. He asked Frank if he could play his music. Frank said, "Yes, I would love to hear you play."

"By the way, my name is Elmore." Man, he could play that guitar. As he played, he slid his hand and fingers up and down that instrument. It was like magic, and you could hear Frank saying, "Man, what a gift God has given you! I really enjoyed you, and thank you for coming." Everyone was sitting on logs or Big Rock. Everyone was eating, singing, dancing, and smiling. It was just a wonderful night.

Now, the big event was about to come on the radio. The radio announcer introduced the beginning of the fight: "In this corner with the black trunks is Jack Dempsey. Fighting out of the other corner wearing the white trunks is light heavyweight Battling Levinsky." During the first round, the announcer gave a blow-by-blow account. You could hear all of the excitement on the radio and also among Frank's friends and family at their get-together.

After two rounds of this event, both fighters came out swinging. The announcer yelled, "It's all over! Battling Levinsky is down. Jack Dempsey has just knocked him out in the third round!" Everyone went wild. What a thrill to hear. The guests at Frank's house were so excited. Everyone had a ball. The guests began to unwind, and then they all started to go home.

Everyone said goodnight to Frank and Martha except for a few who stayed behind to help clean up. Walter Marley and his wife Beatrice stayed to help. The ladies went in the house. Walter walked over to Frank and expressed to him the fun he had had that night. "I can't remember when I have had so much fun," Frank said to Walter.

"I'm glad you had such a good time," Walter said. "You know, I have been wanting to ask you about the last time I saw you, with that other woman that you say you're married to."

"Yes! Man, I know you may not understand. I love them both. I have gotten caught up with these two beautiful women. Now, with Beatrice it is so sweet! Man, when we make love to one another, she gets me what I want. She makes me yell; she takes me to the moon. I just cannot live without her. Yes, the old saying is right: The Blacker the Berry the Sweeter the juice." Walter said this with a big smile on his face. "Now, with Annie life is good. I love her, and I wanted to know what it was like being white. I kind of got pulled in. Being treated so nice, people saying, 'May I help you, sir?' I'm not proud of my actions. I have children with the both of them.

"I have three brothers too; they also look white and, yes, they are married to white women too. You may know my brothers Will Marley, Drew Marley, and Massey Marley. I only see them once in a while. They won't have anything to do with my Black family for the fear of being lynched, yet no one knows that they are also Black men who live their lives as white men."

Frank had sat down on a log as he was listening to Walter. "Man, that is deep. You had better be careful. You know if those white people find out about you, they will try to kill you."

Frank was still taking in everything that had happened that night. The event had been a big success. Now on the porch saying goodnight to Walter and Beatrice and then watching as they pulled down the road making their way home, Frank stood there until he couldn't see them anymore. Martha came outside and held Frank's hand, and then Frank was feeling good. He pulled her closer to him. Then he put his arm around her, holding and kissing her real tight, saying to her, "Baby, I want to make love to you in such a playful manner." She giggled. He started to kiss her on her neck, saying, "Martha, baby, you're going to get it."

Martha says, "Give it to me," as they were making their way to the bedroom. It was hot, both of them pouring with sweat. Frank was on the bed nude. Now Martha was standing up taking off her clothes and then sliding next to her husband. "Say, baby, baby!" But Frank had fallen fast asleep. He was exhausted, over there snoring away. Martha laid there in his arms, falling asleep with him.

Now the year was 1926, and everyone had grown up so big and strong. McKinley was still sweet on Minnie Marley. My, she was now a young lady coming into being a woman. Yes, they were an item--when you saw one, you would see the other.

McKinley would go in the woods for long walks. He would meet Minnie there and they would be there for hours. When his parents asked him what it was he was doing in the woods, he would always say he was just holding Minnie's hand. As he said that, he would have the biggest smile on his face. McKinley's dad told him, "You had better be careful--I know what you are doing. I know one thing: you will marry her if you get her pregnant."

"Dad, we are just holding hands."

Frank says, "Yeah, right."

The year had gone by so fast. It was December now, and McKinley and Minnie were sitting at his parents' kitchen table one day when Minnie told McKinley that something was wrong. She explained to him that she had missed her menstrual cycle.

Well, with this silly look on his face, McKinley said to Minnie, "It will come soon." He was holding the saltshaker in his hand, and he started to tap it on the table out of being nervous. His mother walked into the room and heard the tapping on her table.

"McKinley, would you please stop that tapping on my table."

"Yes, Momma," McKinley said. Then he turned all of his attention back to Minnie, saying, "We will keep this to ourselves, until we know for sure."

Miz Martha asked Minnie, "How is school?   How is your mother doing?"   Minnie answered her, "Oh, everyone is fine. My schoolwork is fine."

"Well, tell your mom I will be cooking Sunday dinner for us. Yes, after church, we are looking forward to spending time with you all catching up on each other. Did McKinley tell you that he will be attending college next year?"   Minnie had a puzzled look on her face and answered, "This is the first time I'm hearing of this."

"Well, yes," Martha said. "He will be done with high school, and it will be time to get that college education started. Besides, it's in his genes." And she proceeded to go on and on about how she adopted McKinley and how his birth parent was educated. She also expressed that God had blessed her with a child, and she couldn't love him any more than if she had given birth to him herself. "I was the first person to hold him. God knew what he was doing. I am grateful. I have delivered so many children, and for whatever reason I was not able to have my own, by birth. So yes, I am truly grateful."

"Now, Momma! I thought we were talking about dinner this coming Sunday."

"Yes, I was, I'm so sorry. I was just reminiscing on my life and wanted to give God all the praise glory!"

Minnie said then, "I love to hear about your life. Yes, I will let my mom know. We have some big news to announce in church this Sunday!"

"Okay!"

McKinley and Minnie walked out the door. Now, on Sunday morning, McKinley went to pick up Minnie in his dad's truck, and then made his way back to pick up his parents so everyone would be on time for church. In the church parking lot, everyone was greeting each other while other people were walking by. McKinley knew that he didn't have much time before church started. He pulled Minnie aside, asking her if she was sure that they were ready for this big announcement.

"Yes, I'm sure," she answered him.

McKinley said, "You know, Minnie, I have loved you from the very day I first laid my eyes on you."

Minnie smiled as McKinley escorted her into the sanctuary. The church was full this morning. McKinley and three others led the church in the morning devotion, standing at the altar one by one praying and giving God all the glory. Now reading from the King James version of the Bible. Pastor White walked in and sat down for a moment. Sitting in the pool pit. Now speaking to his congregation: "Good morning, church!"

Responding back in a very low tone: "Good morning."

Pastor saying, "I know that we can do better than that! I know that we have something to be grateful for. I know that I'm grateful. Now, turn to your neighbor and tell them that God woke you up this morning. So, I'm grateful. Can I get an 'Amen?'"

Church: "I'm thankful. I'm grateful." Now Pastor White had everyone up in their seats, giving a joyous praise. Shouting! Crying, "Yes!" Giving a grateful honor to God.

Pastor White said, "Now, that's how you say a good morning." All of the deacons were in the first row of the church standing and also participating and supporting the pastor.

Now the pastor was calling on the church's secretary. Her name was Hattie Shaw.   Hattie and Minnie were close in age. It was also known that she was sweet on McKinley.   Hattie read all of the announcements. "Also extending a warm and hearty greeting for any visitor that is visiting our church. Now, saying that concludes our announcements."

As she went to sit down, McKinley jumped up and said that he had an announcement. He walked to where Minnie was sitting with her family. McKinley's family was not sitting too far away from them. He grabbed her hand and walked her to the altar to make this announcement. Everyone looking with surprised looks on their faces. Holding Minnie's hand, McKinley said in front of the congregation, "I want to profess my love for Ms. Minnie Marley! I want to ask for Minnie's hand in marriage. So, first, Minnie Marley, will you marry me?" As he got down on one knee, he said, "Will you?"

Minnie was a little quiet, speechless. Then she hugged him and said, "Yes! Yes! Yes! I will marry you." Everyone let out a big gasp and started chattering.

Then McKinley said to his parents, "Mom and Dad, you have raised me to be a man. Now I must cling to my soon-to-be wife. I hope that I have your blessing." His mom was sitting there holding her husband's hand, trying to hold back the tears, nodding yes, and giving her blessing. Now looking over to Minnie's parents, "Mr. and Mrs. Marley, may I have your daughter's hand please, sir and ma'am?"

They both looked at each other. Then Mr. Walter Marley stood up with his hat in his hand, twirling it around because he was a little nervous. Looking over to his sons and his wife Beatrice, he said to McKinley, "Yes. Now, this is my baby girl, and you had better take good care of her."

McKinley said, "Yes, sir, I will." So McKinley, still holding Minnie's hand, shouted out, "Thank you, Lord!"

Pastor White said, "Can the church say 'Amen?' Now that's all right." Now it was time for the pastor to preach. He said, "I think that my sermon is very fitting for what has taken place here today." He was going to talk about Noah. "Let us turn to the Book of Genesis, chapter 6 verse 5. Most of the people on earth were wicked. But Noah and his three sons were righteous. Amen! Now God was sad, because the people were wicked. God told Noah to tell the people to repent. He would send a flood to the earth. God was letting Noah know that he was going to destroy everything and all that was wicked!"

The pastor started putting things in his own words, interpreting from his view. "God says to Noah, 'Gather up and build this ark. Noah, everyone will not really understand why.' Yet Noah trusted in the Lord. Can I get an 'Amen?' I want you to think about that for a moment. God told Noah to build a big boat.

People were passing Noah and laughing at him and his family, saying, 'Oh look, this man is nuts.'

"Now God told Noah, 'When your finish, make sure you have on this boat two of everything.' Okay, telling Noah to close the door on this ark. 'Don't let anyone on once that door is closed!' Amen now, church! It rained for 40 days and 40 nights, yet Noah and everyone on the ark was on this boat for over a year. So, after all of that, God spared Noah from death and saved all that was important. Now, let's talk about what has happened here today! I can feel God telling McKinley about his ark! Making sure he has what is important in starting his family, taking on the responsibilities of life. Amen, keeping the wicked out of your life. Forsaking all others, clinging to your wife." Pastor White had the church up and shouting. He was really preaching! Now Pastor said to the church, "The door of the church is open." Pastor White was greeting everyone and saying his closing for the service. "Now in closing, can we pray? After all of that, church is now dismissed."

Everyone walked out the door and greeted McKinley and his new bride-to-be, Minnie. Now Hattie ran up to McKinley to give him a real big hug, holding on a little too tight, saying to him, "Congratulations." Then, as she let go from her hugging, she looked over to Minnie and said, "I'm so happy for the two of you."

Minnie smiled and stepped between Hattie and McKinley, and stood close to McKinley. She told Hattie that McKinley would be getting the hugs and kisses from her for the rest of their lives. Then she said to McKinley, "We don't want to be late for dinner at your parents' house." She grabbed his hand as the both of them walked away.

Standing by the truck, McKinley said to Minnie, "That was kind of mean. What did you mean by that?"

Changing the subject, Minnie said to McKinley, "Oh, here come Mom and Dad." Minnie said to McKinley, "Don't think I can't see how that Miz Hattie looks at you."

McKinley told Minnie, "I only have eyes for you." Then he kissed her in front of his parents.

Then Miz Martha said, "Oh, this is so sweet."

Now getting in the truck, Frank was driving and McKinley was riding in the back of the truck bed sitting on the toolbox. Minnie was sitting next to her soon-to-be mother-in-law, Miz Martha, who was so excited about the news of her son's engagement. "I hope your parents will make it to the dinner later on this evening," said Miz Martha.

Minnie said, "Yes, ma'am, they will be there along with my brothers. I know that they will all be very hungry."

"Well, I hope so. I made a lot of food."

"What did you make?"

Well, I made some collard greens with ham hocks, homemade potato salad, smoked short ribs, and cornbread. And for dessert, homemade peach cobbler. Minnie, can you cook?"

"Yes, ma'am, I can."

"So, when are the both of you planning on getting married?"

Well, we want to be married by Christmas."

Ms. Martha was taken aback for a moment by this news. Asking, "Why, all of a sudden? That's only in a few weeks."

"Well," Minnie says to Miz Martha, "I may be with child!"

"What? What? Does anyone know about this?"

"Not yet. Well, just you and now your husband. Of course, McKinley." The rest of the ride was quiet until they made it to the house. Frank pulled up to park the truck at the side of the house. McKinley jumped out of the back of the truck to help his mom and fiancée out of the door. Everyone making their way into the house.   Minnie asked Ms. Martha if she could help her set the table. She was also helping with various other thing to make this dinner a grand event. Ms. Martha said, "I really appreciate your help. You know, I'm going to love having a daughter." Minnie smiled.

Frank was outside listening to the news on his radio. McKinley walked up to his dad with this joy in his heart and a pep in his step. "Did you know I have always wanted to marry my Minnie?"

"I know, son. I want you to be happy. I want you to make sure this is what you want."

"Dad, yes, this is what I want."

"Son, you do know that there is more to life than what a woman has between her legs?"

"Dad, I know."

"Son, you don't even have yourself a job. You need a place to live. Have you thought about that?"

"Well, no, Dad!"

"Son, it is called responsibility. I also know the real reason that you're getting married is because Minnie is with child. Isn't that true?"

"Yes, Dad, she may be. We're not a hundred percent sure."

"Son, I'm just saying, your life is real. You have to care for your wife."

"I know, Dad, I will, you will see."

Not too shortly after their conversation, Beatrice and her husband were driving up the street, pulling up in front of the house. All of Minnie's family had come too. Sitting in the back of the truck were her brothers—all four of them--and they looked like they were hungry. Moody said, "Wow, something sure smells good." All of the men stayed in the yard with Frank and McKinley.

Miz Beatrice went into the house. Talking a little loud to get everyone's attention, she said, "Hello! Hello!"

Miz Martha said, "Oh, you all made it! Come on in!" Miz Beatrice gave her daughter a real big hug, then gave Miz Martha one too.

"Look at my baby, she is getting married. I can't even believe it."

"Yes, Momma, I am."

Miz Martha said, "Well, you're going to be a grandmother soon, too."

Miz Beatrice yelled out loud, "What are you talking about?"

Miz Martha said, "You mean, you really didn't know that your daughter is having a baby?"

Answering her, with a bewildered look on her face, "No, I didn't. Minnie, please, please get me a cool drink of water."

Minnie helped her mom sit down first, and then she went to fetch the water. As she made her way back with the water, she asked her mom, "Are you all right?"   "Yes! Yes! I'm fine. It's just, well, I want this evening to go off well. Do me a favor, let us not bring this conversation up anymore today."

Minnie said, "Okay, Momma."

Now Miz Martha said to Minnie, "Sweetie, please go and let everyone know that dinner is ready."

Minnie went out on to the porch to tell the men that dinner was ready. "Everyone, please wash your hands."

The dinner table was very crowded. Frank, being the head of the family, said, "Let us all bow our heads in prayer, so we can give an honor to God. Father God, thank you for this wonderful meal that my wife has prepared for us. In Jesus' name, Amen."

All you could hear was the chatter of pass the meat and the greens, and Johnny saying to Ms. Martha how good the food was. Then Othea said how nice the candle looked on the table.

Ms. Martha said, "Why, thank you." Then nobody was talking at all; you could hear a pin drop.

Then Walter Marley said, "Well the two of you want to get married, huh? Now you know that this is my baby girl. It's going to be very hard to let her go. I mean, I know that I have already given you my blessing. I'm just worried about things. Where are you going to live?"

McKinley said, "Well, sir, I got it all figured out."

"Well, son, I would like to know how."

"Well, Dad! I can call you Dad now, right?"

"Why sure," Walter replied.

"I have already gotten me a job on Mr. Roy Brintal's property. Yes, and a house too. It a start! I will be working on his farm in exchange for our rent. Yes, I will be a sharecropper. Now I know it is not the best job. Yet it is an honest living.   Frank kind of put his head down, saying to everyone, "Now, son, I really wanted better for you."

Dad, I love Minnie, and this is how thing are going to be. I will do better." All of the women in the room were so quiet, listening to the conversation.

Then Ms. Martha said, "Would anyone like dessert? I made some peach cobbler. Everyone said yes! There were two pans of dessert. By the time everyone had been served, each and every drop was gone. Then Walter Marley asked when this wedding was again. Minnie looked over to her dad and she said, "Daddy, I told you on Christmas Day."

Finishing up the night with a drink of moonshine in the yard, Frank and all the males that were there for dinner were now in the yard. With mayonnaise jars as glasses, Frank said, "Raise your glass for a toast. My son, my only child, is getting married! I welcome my new daughter to our family. Congratulations, son." Everyone said at the same time, "Congrats." The rest of the night was full of laughter, jokes, and love.

Now the guests were all gone, and McKinley made sure that Minnie had made it home safely. Frank and his wife had gone to bed, holding his wife in his arms, kissing her. They started a deep conversation about their son. "I sure pray that McKinley takes care of his wife and soon-to-be child," said Frank.

Miz Martha said, "He will be fine. I know that we raised a nice young man. It's time to let him go." Then they fell fast asleep in each other arms.

Now it was Christmas Day. The morning was a bit cool but there no snow. It was the day that Christ was born. Yes! On this day everything and everyone was so quiet. It was as if even the animals knew that it was Jesus' birthday! Miz Beatrice was preparing food for the celebration of Christmas, yet also for the celebration of her only daughter's wedding that day. Minnie saw her mother in the kitchen, while she was standing in the hallway of their home. Peeping around the corner into the kitchen, Minnie said, "Good morning, Mom!"

Miz Beatrice said, "Good morning, baby!"

"You need any help?"

No, sweetie, I think I got this. Now we need to get all of this food to the church. Minnie! Baby! How are you feeling?"

"Momma, I feel fine. We need to make it to church on time. The regular service will be starting at 10:00 AM. The wedding would be shortly after."

Miz Beatrice started to get a little emotional, calling, "Minnie, I don't have much to give you. I have this gift for you."

Minnie's eyes had gotten big and full of tears. "Thank you, Momma," she said, taking the box and then giving her mom a great big hug. She opened the box and saw that it held the only necklace Momma owned. "Mom, I can't take this." "No, baby, I want you to look good on your wedding day."

Standing there holding her mom's hand, Minnie said, "Mom, I love you. Now go get ready!" As Minnie started to walk away, someone was at the door. Minnie answered. It was her uncle Miles.

"Minnie," said her uncle, where is your momma?"

"Oh, she is in the kitchen."

"Okay. I'm here to pick up the food to take it to the church."

"Okay, let me help you put it in your truck," Miz Beatrice said, and they loaded everything up.

As Uncle Miles drove off, he said, "I will see you all later."

The morning started getting busy; everyone was trying to get ready! Later on that morning, now at the church. The place was very crowded. The congregation wanting to give praise to God and to celebrate the birth of Christ. Also, the wedding of McKinley and Minnie! Now looking in from the other room that was across from the sanctuary, Minnie didn't want McKinley to see her before the two of them tied the knot. You could hear the congregation singing, "Oh, Holy Night! Oh, Holy Night!" You could feel the presence of the Holy Spirit. Pastor White had now concluded the service for the Christmas event.

Now the pastor said, "Young McKinley, it's time, young man." McKinley stood up and walked up to the altar. McKinley was standing there in front of the congregation. Standing by his side was his best man, Johnny Marley. The choir director played the piano, playing the musical part of "Amazing Grace." Walking down the aisle first was Mr. and Mrs. Frank Newton as they took their place on one of the seats close to their son. Next walking and being escorted by her son Moody Marley was Miz Beatrice. Moody walked his mother to her seat and gave her a big kiss. Miz Beatrice just had a real big smile on her face and was looking so proud! McKinley was looking so shape and dapper, wearing his best suit. He had on his best tie and his Sunday best shoes.

Pastor White said, "Will the church say Amen?" Now the organist started playing "Here Comes the Bride." Pastor White said, "Would everyone please stand." Standing in the doorway was Walter Marley with his best suit on. Holding on to her dad's arm was Minnie, the most beautiful woman in the world. As the music continued to play, Walter Marley walked his little girl down the aisle. Minnie had on a dress that her auntie Susan Draper had made for her. It was short-sleeved with a soft neckline, showing off the elegant necklace that her mother had given her. She was wearing this candlelight-white dress and also a headband with a veil.

McKinley stood waiting for his bride to make her way to him. He was looking at Minnie just speechless. The pastor said, "Whom giveth this woman to marry this man?"

Walter Marley said, "I do." Giving his daughter a kiss on her cheek, then handing her over to McKinley.

Pastor White said, "We are gathered here to unite this man and this woman in holy matrimony, when a man leaves his mother and father and takes on a wife. God says you must cling to your wife. Now Minnie, you must love and cherish your husband, for richer or poorer, through sickness and in health, forsaking all others till death do you part.

Minnie looked at McKinley and said, "I do."

Pastor White asked McKinley the same thing. McKinley said, "I do."

The pastor had both of the rings in his hand, laying them inside of his Bible. Telling the both of them, "McKinley, take this ring that you have for Minnie. Repeat after me, 'With this ring I thee wed. I give this ring as a toke of my love and affection, so help me God.' Minnie, repeat after me also, say the same words. Then Pastor White said, "Now, by the state of Mississippi and the county of Warren, on this Christmas Day, in the year of 1926, I pronounce you as husband and wife. You may SALUTE YOUR BRIDE. Now, church, may I introduce to you Mr. and Mrs. McKinley Newton."

Both the bride and groom turned around holding each other's hands, with so much excitement and enthusiasm, and then the both of them walked outside. As they greeted their guests, they were smiling and overwhelmed by all the excitement. The hand shaking. The hugs and kisses.

Now there was one that was not happy: Hattie made her way through the crowd, running up to McKinley, putting her arms around his neck, whispering in his ear, "You know that you should have married me." McKinley put some space between the two of them. Minnie looked but was not really concerned, knowing that McKinley had just spoken his undying love and commitment for her. Also knowing that the both of them would soon be parents.

Now walking up to Minnie was one of her brothers--her brother Selvie, and his fiancée Annie Shelton. He was trying to hold back the tears, showing respect for his sister as he congratulated his new brother-in-law. He told McKinley, "Now, you know this is my little sister. I know that you will always take good care of her." McKinley said, "Yes, always." Then he took Minnie's hand and said, "Oh, Minnie, it's time for us to go inside for our wedding dinner."

Inside the church, the communion room was festive for the occasion, for both Christmas and their wedding. The flowers were so pretty. On the far side of the room was a smorgasbord of food that Minnie's mom and the congregation had prepared. Pastor White was standing at the front of the room. He said, "Everyone, please bow your heads so we can give an honor to God. Father God, we would like to say thank you. Thank you, Lord, for this day, for us recognizing the birth of your son, Jesus Christ, that you sent down here to earth to save us from our sins so that we could have another chance at everlasting life. Father, we would like to thank you for bringing these two young people together in holy matrimony. Also, Father, that they will be fruitful and multiply as they start their new journey together as one. Father, please bless all that have taken part in the preparation of the food that we are about to eat. We all ask these things in Jesus' holy name. Amen. Now, let us eat because the food looks so good."

The servers that were standing behind the table had made sure that McKinley and Minnie were served first, and also that the pastor's meal was brought to him too. Now that everyone was served and eating, the room was full of chatter and laughter. The day was getting late. It was time for McKinley to take his bride home to his parents' house where they would be staying for a few weeks while their home was being repaired. So, for the new year that was fast approaching, everyone pitched in to make sure that the new couple had a place that they could call home. Even if it was on the property of Mr. Roy Brintal.

The New Year was here—1927. Calvin Coolidge was the 30th president of the United States of America. He was a one-term President. He did not run for office a second time because of the death of his son, Cal, Jr. His death took a heavy toll on the president and led him into a deep clinical depression. Also in the year of 1927, there was the Great Mississippi Flood. It was one of the most destructive floods of all times. Over 500 people lost their lives in this flood. Down in the delta of Mississippi, more that 200,000 African Americans were displaced from their homes, most being forced to live in relief camps for a long period of time. Not getting the help that so many of them needed. As a result of this disruption of their everyday lives, many migrated to the north to live much better, moving to a better place where there was more work in industry. Where African Americans could for the first time have themselves some independence.

The people that stayed in Mississippi that needed help to make ends meet had received help from the NAACP, with their support, warning of the harsh living conditions. Also, there was mistreatment of Black laborers within the camps.

In April of 1927, McKinley and Minnie had lost everything. They had only been living in their new home for a few months, and the flood had taken all that they had worked so hard for. Minnie had started to show as her stomach had gotten larger. Now being a little more than five months pregnant, they needed a place to stay until the living conditions were fit, to live in. Until everything dried out, they would not be able to live in the home that really belonged to Roy Brintal. They were able to move back into the house of McKinley's parents, Miz Martha and Frank Newton, because it had not been affected by the flood.

McKinley was working very hard on the land trying to get the crops in order, with so many others that worked and lived on the land. There were approximately 50 homes on this property. Every morning, McKinley would kiss his wife goodbye in the home that was assigned to them. One day on his way to work in the fields, McKinley could hear Mr. Brintal say to one of the leading workers to subtract from the pounds that everyone had picked. Example: If they picked 10 pounds of cotton, then tell them that they only picked 7 pounds of cotton. So that everyone would work much harder. Now McKinley didn't let his lead man know that he was aware of their deception, even though McKinley knew of their unfair work ethic. It just made him work harder. He also wanted to put himself in a better position.

One day after work, McKinley made a point in going to see one of the local bankers in town, Mr. Will Montgomery. Yes, a very respectable man. Yes, sitting there waiting real patiently for Mr. Montgomery who was with another customer. Now he was done, as he escorts them to the door. Now he looked over and saw McKinley sitting there. He said to McKinley, "Hey there, how have you been? Were you waiting on me?"

McKinley said, "Yes, sir!"

"Well, come on in my office. Now, what can I help you with?"

Well sir, we mean me, and my wife were affected by the flood. We are expecting our first baby soon. We are staying with my parents until we can get our place together. I'm renting from Mr. Brintal in exchange for my work as a sharecropper. I guess, I was wondering if you have any information on some new employment and possibly a loan?"

"Well, McKinley, there will be some new jobs coming this way soon. Now it will only be temporary, maybe a year at the most. You have to fill out an application. The job is working on construction putting in new roads throughout the cities. The pay is really good. Real good money!

Now, about the loan. There are federally funded development programs that will help low-income families get on their feet. Take the time to apply, and you will hear from me soon. After about 20-30 minutes filling out these applications, McKinley turned them in to Mr. Montgomery, telling him thank you. "You are a good man."

"Well, that is what I'm here for, to help people. You will hear from me soon."

Walking out of the door and into the truck his dad had passed down to him, McKinley was in a very good mood. Now on his way home for the day! As he pulled up at his parents' house, parking the truck in the front of their home, McKinley opened up the door and walked over to his mom, then to his wife, giving them both a big kiss. Miz Martha said, "WOW! Someone is in a very good mood."

Saying to his mom about the events of the day, "You know, this flood was like nothing that I've ever seen. It's going to be months before we will see things back to normal. I had a talk with Mr. Montgomery at the bank. So, it won't be too long before we will be back into our own place. Beside that, our baby will be here soon. I'm working real hard trying to pull things together."

"I know you are, son. They are using prisoners to do the labor that some of these people could do but won't. The government uses them for free labor, putting them to work to build the levees and flood walls to prevent future floods." Ms. Martha was telling her son, "Well, that is not fair."

No, Mom, it's not, some of these young men could get out here and make some money. They are letting their pride stand in the way of taking care of business. There was a knock at the door. McKinley answered the door. It was his brother-in-law Selvie (nicknamed Marley). "Hey there, Marley," said McKinley. "How are you doing? Come on in." Selvie, who was light complexioned and stood about 5 feet 8 inches tall, walked in the door. If you didn't know his family, you might think he had a Hispanic background.

Selvie spoke to his sister and then to Miz Martha. Then Selvie asked his brother-in-law, McKinley, "What you got going on later this evening?"

"Oh, not much just dinner, and then I'm getting ready for bed. You know I have to go to work in the morning."

"Well, I was wondering if you could go with me this Saturday," asked Salvie.   "Where?"

"It's this place that's up in the woods where you can unwind. Also, you can get yourself some good food. I also go there to see who wants to play the numbers for the day."

"Now, Marley, you know that I don't participate or go to places like that.   I'm ready for church on Sunday."

Marley didn't give up. "Come on, man, we won't be there too long. You can shoot pool. It won't interfere with your daily routine."

So McKinley finally said, "Okay, I will go to keep you company. But only for a short time. He said this as Marley was making his way to the door.

Marley said, "Bye, Minnie. Bye, Miz Martha."

McKinley walked outside with Marley and said, "I will see you this weekend."   "Okay," Marley replied. As he was pulling off in his truck, McKinley went back in the house and then enjoyed the rest of his evening with his mom and his wife.

Now Saturday had arrived. The sun was shiny bright. In the house, you could smell the bacon and eggs cooking, along with the homemade biscuits and grits, and the coffee percolating on the stove. Minnie was up cooking for her husband. Yes, with her hand on her hip, trying to provide some support to her back, because of being pregnant. McKinley got up and made his way to the kitchen. He walked up behind Minnie and put his arms around his wife, telling her good morning, how much he loved her, and also how he appreciated everything that she did, and that she would never have to work a day in her life. "I will always do my best to take care of you and our family, Minnie. I want to have a big family too."

"Oh, McKinley," Minnie answered as she smiled. Then both of them sat down to enjoy their breakfast. Miz Martha and Frank had gone out early that morning to pick up supplies for their everyday needs. When Minnie and McKinley had finished breakfast, McKinley had some time on his hands and helped Minnie clean up the kitchen and put things away. Minnie said to her husband, "Are you still going with Marley to his juke joint?"

"Now, Minnie! You know I don't want to, yet I told him that I would. Minnie replied, "Well, please keep an eye on him."

"Now, Minnie, you know I will." The day was going by real fast. Coming down the street in his truck was Selvie Marlcy.

"Hey, McKinley! Are you ready to go?"

McKinley said, "Hold on, let me get my hat." Fortunately, his mom and dad had returned from their shopping. McKinley didn't like leaving Minnie unless he knew that there was someone at the house with her, knowing that she could go into labor with their first child at any time. Now he kissed Minnie and said to her, "I will see you later." Marley was outside standing beside his truck, talking to Frank Newton. Marley was dressed really well in nice slacks and a dress shirt, and his hair was combed back. He was a very handsome young man.

"So," Frank said, "What are the both of you getting into today?"

Selvie Marley answered, "Oh, not much, going to get some lunch at these new places up in the woods. I hear they have some good catfish."

Now Frank said, "You guys should be careful."

McKinley had on his everyday hat and his denim overalls, and he told his dad not to worry about them and he would be home soon. McKinley and Selvie got into the truck and began making their way down the road, heading to this juke joint. Selvie was feeling good in spirit, and pulled out of his pocket what looked like a hand-rolled cigarette. He put it into his mouth and took out his lighter so he could smoke his cigarette. Selvie took a few puffs and then tried to hand his smoke over to McKinley. McKinley said, "I don't smoke that wacky tobacco. Where did you get that stuff from?"

Selvie answered, "Man, whatever you need, I can get it for you. I also run the lottery numbers every day."

McKinley said, "Man, you act like you are the cities of Edwards and Vicksburg Pharmaceutical. I know you need to be careful before you end up in jail."
Selvie started driving faster, yes, he was high feeling good!

The road was long and winding, and they finally made it to the juke joint. Getting out of the truck, both of them could smell the fish frying! People were standing outside doing side deals. A few ran up to Selvie Marley. "Hey, Marley, you got what I need?"

Marley said, "I got you, man!" McKinley and Marley walked inside the juke joint. You could hear the music playing-- they were playing the blues. A few people were dancing really close to each other, gyrating their hips. Everyone seemed to know Marley. As he walked through the building, he introduced his brother-in-law to some of the people that he knew. Now at the back of this place was the kitchen where a woman was cooking. Marley said, "Hey, Miss Lady!"

She replied, "Hey, how are you?" This lady had a real big smile on her face. She would serve moonshine too. Marley asked her, "Hey, can we have two drinks?" The woman said, "Yes!"

As Marley was pulling out his money to pay for the drinks, another woman walked up to him asking whether it was too late to put her lotto number in. "No," Marley said. "What's the number you want to play?"

She said, "I want to play 586 for 10 cents in the box." Marley took her number down, and a few others played too. Now both Marley and McKinley sat down at a table and ordered two catfish dinners. They were enjoying the music and waiting for their meals, and Marley was drinking one glass after another of moonshine. At this point, Selvie Marley was just downright plastered and was not able to keep his composure.

McKinley said to Marley, "Are you alright? Marley looked at him and spoke in another language that no one could understand. It was pig Latin.

The cook came from behind the counter to bring them their dinners. She walked toward the table to set the dinners down and asked McKinley, "Is he going to be okay?"

McKinley said, "Yes, I believe so."

She said, "Well, I hope you enjoy your meals."

Marley went on for about an hour talking out of his head, being very annoying to all that were in his presence. Then a man walked over from the other side of the room--he had had enough of this nonsense. He was telling Marley to shut the fuck up! McKinley was now watching to make sure Marley was okay. Then Marley stood up to tell this man to go to hell. Then, with all of this courage, Marley pushed this man. Trying to keep Marley from getting his ass kicked was his brother-in-law McKinley. This man stood about 6 feet 5 inches. Yes, he was getting the best of them. Glasses were flying, chairs were being thrown around. Everything was out of control.

Then out of nowhere came the lady from behind the counter. She was amazing--it was like she was a man. She was knocking out these men. This lady put things back in control. Talking in this large voice: "If you don't like it, you can get the hell out of here. Don't make me hurt anyone." Marley and McKinley were trying to pull things together. The lady walked over to Marley and asked, "Are you alright?" and she helped him up off of the floor. She finally said to Marley, "My name is Stella, and I would really like to get to know you."

McKinley was trying to make sense of what had just transpired, still in a state of shock. Marley was still intoxicated, yet in a playful mood, and he lay his head on Stella's breast, telling Stella that he could do some real sexual things to her. Looking at Stella, the only way that you knew that she was a woman was the fact that she had large breasts. Marley put his head between her breasts, making a gurgling sound and saying to McKinley that she would take him home with her. Stella got McKinley's address and said, "I will drop him off in the morning when he sobers up."

McKinley picked up Marley's keys and told him, "I can drive you him home."

Marley said, "No, I know what I'm doing. I will see you tomorrow." McKinley said, "Okay. You know that your sister won't like this."

"Oh, now, I'm going to get me some pooh-tang! Yes, some Black pooh-gang." McKinley couldn't convince Marley to go home with him. So, he drove his truck back to his parents' house. Going in the house, he had to explain to his wife what had happened this night and the behavior of her brother.

Minnie wasn't pleased at all, saying to her husband, "You shouldn't have left him there," stressing her concern about Marley's well-being.

McKinley said, "Sweetie, it will be all right now," as he fell fast asleep.

Now it was Sunday morning, and Minnie was up again, cooking breakfast for everyone. Yes, it was kind of what her job was, taking on this responsibility on her own. Up next were her mother-in-law and father-in-law. Minnie was explaining to them what her husband had told her about the previous night. McKinley was still sleeping and Minnie was getting all of their things ready for church which started at 11:00 AM. It was only around 8:30 at the present time.

In the midst of their conversation, they heard a faint knock at the door. It was her brother Marley. There was this woman that stood behind him. She was not attractive at all. Marley walked in with this person with a serious look on his face, as if she had put him in his place. He said, "Good morning."

Minnie said, "Good morning."

Marley introduced Stella to his sister and to Mr. And Mrs. Newton. Minnie asked Stella, "Would you like a cup of coffee?"

Stella said, "Yes, thank you, that would be nice."

Minnie said, "Thank you for bringing my brother home safe. I really don't know what gets into him when he is drinking that moonshine." Stella then expressed that everyone would be seeing a whole lot more of her. Stella had made love to Marley and she was love-struck. Marley this and Marley that--every word out of her mouth was about Selvie Marley. Now Minnie was thinking, Did her brother bother to tell this woman he was a married man?

Miz Martha and Frank were all dressed up, getting ready for church. McKinley was also up and dressed for church. Minnie said that she wasn't going to church that day, not wanting to leave Marley and Stella at the house. Also, Minnie was a little tired and her feet were swollen. After a long conversation with the both of them, Stella finally told Marley that she would see him a little later and both Minnie and Marley said goodbye to Stella.

Shortly after her leaving, Minnie asked her brother, "What are you doing? I know you remembered that you're a married man."

Marley said, "Yes, I don't really know what happened. I know one thing led to another. I woke up this morning, and I thought I was in bed with a man. Whew! It scared me so bad."

"You know what? You're starting to act like Dad!"

"Who, me?"

"Yes, you. I know that Dad has another family that lives in Yazoo. I know that we have a sister. I'm not sure if she knows about us. Also, they go for being a white family. A lot of people don't know that dad is Negro, especially in Yazoo. I'm just afraid that one day someone will find out and they will hurt him. All that drinking the both of you do. It's like you become another person, like you get this big dose of courage. I know that you and Dad have to be more mindful that you're only one person and a very small man at that. Promise me you will do better at getting your life together."

"Yes, sis, I promise."

"Your truck is outside. Here are your keys. Please go home to your wife. I know that she is worried about you."

"Okay, sis. I will see you soon. I love you."

"I love you, too."

Marley walked out the door to his truck. As he drove off, Minnie watched him ride down the dirt road until she couldn't see him anymore.

Approximately four weeks had gone by which made it the end of September. McKinley was still busy working, still attending Sunday School and church faithfully. His wife at this present time was bedridden. It was a Monday. Minnie always wanted to make McKinley's breakfast every day, even if she was to stay in bed. This morning was a little different. Yes! She had achieved her task! Shortly after serving her husband his breakfast,

McKinley said, "Minnie I'm done with our home. We will be able to move in soon. I'm hoping for this weekend. I just need to clear things with Mr. Roy Brintal. I need to know how much work I have to do for the rent. Because of his unfair tactics, I just don't want to be taken advantage of."

Minnie was sitting down listening to her husband. She stood up and her water had broken. It was like someone had a big bucket of water under her dress. The water went everywhere. Minnie looked at McKinley and he was looking back at her. Their eyes were so big, like what should we do? McKinley took Minnie's hand to assist her to sit down. He said, "Are you alright?"

She said, "Yes, I'm okay!"

It was a good thing that Miz Martha was just in the other room. She had delivered so many babies as a midwife. This was the first time she would deliver her own grandchild. McKinley yelled out to his Mother, "Mom! Mom! It's time! It's time!" Miz Martha came into the kitchen where they were. She could see that the floor was wet and that both Minnie and McKinley were a little scared. Miz Martha took Minnie by the hand and walked her to the room she would use for the birthing room. She also let her husband Frank know to stand by just in case they had to make their way to Jackson to the local hospital.

Ms. Martha told her son, "Sweetheart, I'm going to help Minnie get into a nice clean gown. I'm not sure how long this will take because this is her first time for giving birth. Miz Martha asked Minnie, "How are you feeling?"

Minnie said, "I'm fine," as she lay there resting, not sure what would happen next. Two hours had gone by asking Minnie the same thing. Still nothing. Miz Martha told McKinley to let Minnie's mother and father know that Minnie would soon be in labor. Also stressing that it would be a very long night. It was already after 6:00 PM already!

Miz Beatrice and her husband came over and were in Miz Martha's living room, going back and forth from the room with their daughter to the porch, nervous. McKinley was back in the birthing room with his wife. Every hour checking on Minnie. Still nothing. No labor yet. Miz Martha was starting to get a little concerned. It was now 10 PM. Miz Martha told McKinley to go into the next room where his mother-in-law and father-in-law were sitting.

Miz Martha expressed her feelings on the fact that Minnie had not gone into labor. "I don't want to put them in any danger. So, I think that we should take Minnie to the hospital."

As soon as she finished her sentence, Minnie let out a real big yell. "Oh! I'm in pain. Oh, this hurts so bad."

Miz Martha said to McKinley, "Son, get back there and hold her hand." Miz Martha went to check on Minnie. After giving her a pelvic check, Miz Martha said, "We still have a way to go. The good news is we don't need to go to hospital now!" The pain that Minnie was experiencing was getting closer each time. At first her pain was just ten minutes apart. Now the pain was five minutes apart.

The night was long, yet no one had sleep on their minds. Checking on Minnie time after time. It was now 5:00 AM in the morning. Miz Martha checking on her daughter-in-law again, being really careful. Miz Martha saying, "I can feel the baby's head, so it won't be long." McKinley was sitting right by his wife's side while Minnie slipped in and out of sleep from being extremely exhausted from labor. Now two more hours had gone by. Miz Martha checked on Minnie, and then looked over to her son. "McKinley, wake up! Wake up, it's time! Here we go."

At this time Miz Beatrice came into the room to help her daughter. It went by so fast. McKinley was holding one of Minnie's legs, and Miz Beatrice had the other leg. Miz Martha said to Minnie, "Breathe. Come on, you can do it. I see the baby's head coming through."

Minnie yelled out, "I can't do this."

Everyone was saying at the same time, "Yes, you can. The hardest part is coming, the baby's shoulders are pushing through." Miz Martha now had the baby in her hands. Not sure yet of the gender of the baby? Everyone was anticipating finding out what it was. Finally, Miz Martha said, "It's a girl! Yes, it's a girl!" Miz Martha wrapped the baby up in a sterile blanket, nice and warm, and handed this beautiful baby with a head full of hair to her mother, so much in a state of blissful joy. Minnie was holding on to her bundle of joy as she put her head next to her own mother's. Miz Beatrice said to her daughter, "My baby is now a mother!" McKinley couldn't wait to hold his little baby before he had to leave for work. Miz Martha walked into the other room to get both Frank and Walter to come into the birthing room to share in the joy. Minnie and McKinley's parents were so elated about the birth of their very first grandchild.

Miz Martha had to write down important information about the birth of the baby: the time, the date, the weight, and also the baby's name. She asked the new parents, "What's the baby's name?"

"Well! I will let you know after I wake up. I'm so very tired," answered Minnie.

"Okay, you have plenty of time," said Miz Martha. The grandparents carried the baby into the other room, and took turns holding her. Saying how beautiful she was. Also, how bright her complexion was.

"I know one thing," Walter Marley said, "this one will be very spoiled. I will give her everything that she wants." Everyone was glowing! Proud grandparents all the way around.

Now Minnie was very tired from being up all night and because she had just given birth to her first child. Her mom stayed until Minnie had woken up and then brought her baby back to her, telling her how proud she was that Minnie had given birth to her first grandbaby. "Minnie, sweetie, how are you feeling?"

"Well, Mom, I feel okay, still a little tired." Miz Beatrice said that she would stay a few days to help her only daughter. Minnie was grateful to her mother for showing her how to take care of her child.

Miz Martha walked in the room where Minnie was and said, "Now, I need to get a name for your daughter. So what have the both of you decided?"

"McKinley is not here right now," answered Minnie, "but we have decided to name our firstborn after the day me and McKinley got married. Yes, this is as close as we could get to Christmas. Her birthday is September 27, 1927. So, we are naming her Christine Newton."

Miz Martha said, "I love it--Christine!"

Miz Beatrice said, "Yes, I love it too."

"Well, it's official," said Miz Martha. Now I need to turn this birth certificate in to the county clerk's office. Oh, Minnie, McKinley told me that your house is all ready for you to move back into, but I want you to know that you can stay here as long as you need to."

"I know, Momma. You have been so nice to me."

"Baby, you're the daughter I never had. I love you so much."

"I love you too."

Minnie's mom also said to the both of them, with a smile on her face, "I love you all too." For the rest of the day, Minnie shared her baby with her parents. When the day had come to an end, McKinley returned home from a long day of work and told everyone about the events of the rest of his day. McKinley shared the fact that he had run into Mr. Will Montgomery. Mr. Montgomery had stopped by the field where many men worked to tell them about a new employment opportunity: the construction of new roads and highways running from one city to the next.

"Well, it look like I will have a new job in a few weeks," said McKinley.

Minnie said to her husband, "Oh, this is great news."

"Yes, it is," McKinley said, speaking back to his wife. Now where is my little girl?" Minnie handed the baby to McKinley who held his baby, smiling at her. Talking to her in a baby voice. "I'm going to give my baby the world. Yes, Daddy will work hard for you, sweetie." The rest of the night was spent playing quietly and joking around with his wife. "Now, you know this weekend we will be moving into our own house."

Minnie said, "Yes, I know, McKinley. I just want to rest right now." As a family, they all turned in for the night.

A new day! A new month, a very new beginning. Even though Minnie had just given birth to their baby, she was up cooking breakfast for her husband. The morning was crisp. The sun was shining. McKinley was feeling like a million dollars, feeling rich with love for his brand-new baby. With love for his wife. With the love he had for his parents. With the love for family and friends and from his church. He walked up behind his wife and put his arms around her waist, kissing her the neck.

Minnie started to giggle, telling him, "Your mom and dad are in the next room!"

McKinley said, "You are right. We need to get our things and move into our own house." Just as the both of them had started to eat their food, there was a knock on the door. It was their Uncle Miles!

"Hey, how's everyone doing? Let me see the new baby. I can't believe it, I'm a great uncle. Aww, look at her, she is just absolutely beautiful. What did you name her?"

"We named her Christine Newton," McKinley said, adding how proud the both of them were for being new parents.

"Well, I'm here, of course, to see my great-niece. McKinley, I told you that I would help you move into your home when it was ready, so I'm here to help."

"Oh, okay, yes! I'm just finishing up on my breakfast. Would you like something to eat?"

"Oh, no. But I will take a cup of coffee."

"Sure, no problem." McKinley was talking things over with Uncle Miles about their move.

Uncle Miles said to McKinley, "I know that you have to get a start in life. I'm just not that comfortable with you doing any business with Roy Brintal. He is a slave driver! I know they say that slavery is over, but I can't tell when it comes to him. He treats all of his workers like crap. Making sure that you address him with 'Yes, sir,' or to his wife, 'Yes, ma'am.' It has even been said that Roy Brintal has fathered some children being born to some of these unwed mothers. When you ask them where the father of these children is, they become quiet, not wanting to get in trouble or even be evicted from their homes."

Now, right before McKinley and Uncle Miles had gotten ready to leave, Frank Newton came into the kitchen. "Hey, Miles. How have you been?"

"Oh, Frank, I'm fine. I'm here to help your son move to his newly repaired place. I was also telling him about Mr. Roy Brintal."

"Oh, yes, I know what you mean. I don't like it either. I think that McKinley is trying to follow in my footsteps. This is where we got our start. Me and my wife, Martha, have been in this house for so long. This house has sentimental value. Yes, we were sharecroppers once upon a time. We consider ourselves to be smart about it, with the fact of my wife, Miz Martha, being a midwife. As for me, I no longer do any sharecropping for Mr. Roy Brintal. We have bought this house outright, contract and all, yes, sir! We have a deed to this house. Yes, we are homeowners. To make sure everything was on the up and up, I went to the bank and had Mr. Will Montgomery draw up the legal papers. I have also been working with the railroad."

Uncle Miles said, "Yes, that is a great thing to hear. Okay, McKinley, let's get this show on the road."

McKinley said, "Okay," and kissed Minnie and his baby girl.

"Oh, son, before you leave, I have a few things to give you," said his father. I'm giving you a cow and a rooster to wake you up in the morning. He has six hens, and trust me, son, they will have so many baby chicks. This will keep eggs and milk on the table. If you want, I have a few pigs too.

McKinley said, "Thank you, Dad."

"I will deliver the animals later on today, as soon as I get back from taking your mother shopping in town."

"Okay, Dad, see you soon." Uncle Miles and McKinley made their way out the door. They were on their way with almost all of McKinley and Minnie's belongings in Uncle Miles's truck. Now they were coming down the road! Their house sat back, almost hidden in the tall, green grass. The house seemed to be sitting in nowhere land. There were no houses close to it. There were other houses on this land, but they were approximately a mile away from their house. As they approached McKinley's new home, from afar the house looked like it was a pale blue. The structure seemed a little unsteady as well.

Uncle Miles said to McKinley, "I think we need to check this house's foundation. You know I wouldn't feel right if I didn't!"

McKinley said, "Yes, you are right. I know you are a carpenter by trade." The both of them got out of the truck, and with his toolbox in his hand, Uncle Miles walked up three steps to the porch. He began checking the porch for rotten wood as well as measuring the size of the porch.

Uncle Miles said to McKinley, "I can fix this. Let's go inside." He still had his measuring tape in his hand as he walked in the door, peering into the living room. Uncle Miles looked up at the ceiling, checking the frame, saying, "Oh, yes, there is work to be done here."

McKinley said, "I don't have the experience, but I'm willing to learn."

"Yes, you will have a chance to get some experience under your belt. You can move your things in here, but I don't think you should move your family in until I can make a few more repairs. McKinley said that he agreed. McKinley went out to the truck to gather up his belongings and began putting everything in its place. Soon it was time to leave and go back to his parents' house. McKinley spent the rest of the day explaining to his dad and his mom and his wife the reasons that they wouldn't be moving in right away. Now the night had come and gone.

Now it was a few weeks later, and McKinley had just moved his family into their very repaired home. Minnie's parents and her were there, trying to help out in any way that they could. Also, McKinley's parents were there too. Everything had gotten done, from making sure the outhouse was clean to putting curtains on the windows, to feeding the chickens that ran around in the yard. The baby had a homemade bassinet which was placed in Minnie and McKinley's bedroom.

Frank said, "Son, I know that you're going to start your new job on Monday." McKinley said, "Yes, Dad. I will be working in construction. I'm real excited about it too. I know that this job is temporary, and I know that I will also have to keep my other job as a sharecropper. Yes, there would be very long nights, but I have to do like you, Dad, and make a way for my family." Everyone enjoyed themselves at McKinley and Minnie's new home. They made their way out of the door, and Minnie and McKinley settled themselves, all tucked in for the night.

Now Monday was here. McKinley was up before Minnie had gotten out of bed. McKinley was cooking breakfast for his wife. Minnie walked into the kitchen and saw her husband cooking. She said, "Wow, this is a surprise. I should be up cooking for you."

McKinley said, "Oh, Momma, I want to do something special for you. Minnie, I love you."

Minnie said, "I love you too." Now McKinley was all ready to go. He had his lunch in his hand. He yelled out to his wife that he was about to leave as he was walking in her direction because he always gave Minnie a kiss for the start of his day.

McKinley was to report to the bank. When he got there, he was directed to another room in the back of the bank. In this room were about 30 other men waiting and wanting to know what this job consisted of. Mr. Will Montgomery walked in. He said, "Good morning! Good morning. Thank you all for showing up. Let me start by saying that this job is not for the weak at heart. This job will be hard. Yes, very hard work. So, if anyone feels this isn't for them, please leave now. I will understand." One man stood up and thanked Mr. Montgomery for giving him the opportunity. Then he walked out the door. Mr. Montgomery asked again, but this time no one got up.

"Okay, great," continued Mr. Montgomery. "Well, men, we will be building roads that lead to other cities and also highways. We will be breaking up rock with sledgehammers, carrying big rocks, and moving dirt from one place to another. I'm going to pass this list around. I want you to put your name and address on this list so we can make sure that everyone gets paid on time. You will sign in each and every morning. Now, there are only 29 of you here today. You all will be assigned to what we call a foreman or a head man on the job. Also, not wanting a lot of vehicles on the job site, you will park your car or truck here in the back of the bank. Everyone will be dropped off where they are to work." There was some mumbling amongst the men in the room. Then Mr. Montgomery began calling out names to tell them who they would be working with.

McKinley's boss was named Robert. Robert introduced himself and told his group to meet him outside and be ready to go. "Also," he added, "each and every morning, we would be leaving here at 8:00 AM sharp. Oh, by the way, you only see a group of six men here now, but I will be adding six new men a day to lighten and load and spread out the work. This job at hand is part of a federally funded job. We will be touching city to city with one rock at a time to make the roads meet. Okay, men, let's get this job done!"

Now of course, Robert was a white man. You all can call me Bob," he said. When they got to the job site, Bob told everyone, "Today, we are going to move rubbish and trees, making this area smooth so we can make a road here eventually."

McKinley and the other five men got out of the truck. Everyone was working, moving everything that was in the way. Putting things on the truck to move out of the area. After working about three hours straight, Bob blew his whistle to let everyone know it was time for lunch. McKinley made his way to the truck. There was a special place on the side of this truck where their lunches were stored. Most everyone sat together to eat their lunch. But not Bob. He would sit inside the work truck. McKinley and the other five men sat on big rocks or tree stumps. Now giving each other an informal introduction, McKinley couldn't help seeing that one man in particular kept looking at him. McKinley couldn't help himself. He said, "Hi, my name is McKinley."

The other man said, "Hi, my name is Jonathan Brooks, Jr." Wow, that name sounded so familiar! "I couldn't help looking at you. You look like this man that lives around our family. His name is Mr. Henry Nixon. He was a professor at Alcorn University. Man, you two could be twins." Jonathan said that he had heard that this man was the father of a young man who lived in this area. "Now, what are the chances it would be you?" Not letting on that he had heard about the man Jonathan was talking about, McKinley just let him keep talking. Then Jonathan said, "Wait a minute. You said your name is McKinley."

McKinley said, "Yes, that would be me."

"My mother gave birth to a son named McKinley in 1906 in August."

"What is your mother's name?"

"Well, my mother died in 1908 giving birth to a baby that was breeched."

Not wanting to give anything away, McKinley just listened. Then, really slowly, he asked, "What was your mother's name?"

Jonathan said to him, "Her name was Lola Hood. She was married to my father, so Lola Brooks. I'm here because my auntie Seal and my uncle Willie Earl told me about this job. So, I applied."

McKinley was holding an apple in his hand. While listening to what Jonathan had to say, he dropped it on the ground. McKinley, with this stunned look on his face, said, "I'm not sure, but I believe that you are my brother. My birth mother's name was Loula Hood, and she died at the house that my parents live in today! My parents took me as their own child after she wanted to throw me into the river."   Now Jonathan was in a state of disbelief. "You know that we have different fathers."

"Yes, I know. Man! Man! Wow! I didn't believe that this would ever happen."

Jonathan was saying, "If you want, I can get you information on Mr. Henry Nixon. I know some of his family members. When I see you again, I will have a phone number so you can do what you want with it. Man, I'm so happy I met you!" They hugged each other with a sense of joy.

Now lunch was over, back to work. Everyone worked very diligently for the next five hours until it was time to stop working. They had worked some long hours.   Bob, the lead man, called everyone together. He loaded up the truck and gave a ride back to the bank parking lot where everyone had parked their vehicles. Now Bob was yelling out to his crew, "Be here at 8:00 AM sharp! Have a good night!"

McKinley said to his brother, Jonathan, "Would you like to come over for dinner? Also, if you need a place to stay, you could sleep on the sofa."

Jonathan said, "Well. thank you for your invite, but I have plans already. I will see you bright and early tomorrow morning. Oh, I will have that information for you about your birth dad."

McKinley said, "I'm looking forward to spending time with you."

"Oh, okay, me too!" And they walked away from each other.

McKinley was so excited about the fact that he had met his brother. He couldn't wait to get home to tell his wife. McKinley pulled up to his house, got out of his truck, and ran up the stairs and into the house. Yelling to Minnie, "You won't believe what happened today."

Minnie said to McKinley, "What? What happened? How was your day? Calm down. What are you so excited about?"

"Well, you won't believe this. I ran into my birth brother! He's working with me on the job site. We talked about our birth mother. His name is Jonathan, Jonathan Brooks. Yes, our birth mother's name was the same, Lola Hood. He even knows the name of my birth father, Henry Nixon."

"McKinley, maybe you need to talk this over with your mother. I'm sure that she has a lot of information on this matter."

"Well, I don't want to hurt my mom's feelings. She will always be my mom. I just want to know where I come from is all."

"I can understand. Now, let me fix your dinner. It is ready." Minnie brought McKinley his dinner. McKinley talked the rest of the night about his brother until it was time to turn in.

Minnie had just put baby Christine to sleep. Minnie was sitting on the bed brushing her hair. McKinley said to his wife, "Here, let me help you brush your hair. He brushed her hair for a while. Then he smelled her hair and began telling her how good her hair smelled. Minnie smiled at him. He put his face next to

Minnie's face and started giving her slow, soft kisses. Kissing her lips. Kissing her ears. Kissing her neck. Kissing down her back. Now on her breast. They both began to moan, feeling the passion between them. The thrust of an erection as McKinley made love to his wife. This went on for the duration of the night! After the passion of the night had stopped, McKinley held his wife until the morning had come.

Now after doing the everyday task of getting ready for work, McKinley made it to his work site on time. It was 8:00 AM and everyone was on the truck ready to go. McKinley was looking around for Jonathan, but he was nowhere to be found. Of course, McKinley was disappointed that his brother had not shown up. Making it to the work site, the crew began to work. McKinley was working hard all morning, wondering what could have happened to his brother.

After working for about two hours, another crew of twelve men was dropped off at the work site where McKinley was assigned to work. McKinley looked at the new crew but wasn't really paying attention to who was being dropped off at the site. But then Jonathan walked up to McKinley, saying to him, "Hey, Mack."

McKinley was so happy to see his brother that they instantly started to hug one another for a very brief moment. McKinley said to his brother, "Man, I thought for a minute you may have quit."

"No! Not me. I need this money. I have a lot of things I need to do! Oh, before I forget, I have that information on getting in touch with Henry Nixon. Here is a phone number for a sister of his. I know that she lives in Memphis, Tennessee. I believe her name is Aretha Nixon. I had my auntie Seal contact her. She will be waiting on your call."

McKinley told his brother, "Thank you, man. Thanks a lot. But now we had better get back to work."

Jonathan said, "Yes, you're right."

Later on that day after getting off work, McKinley said goodbye to his brother. The both of them wouldn't be working together for the rest of the month. Yet they did make it a point to stay in touch with each other. McKinley put all of his time into his work for the next few months.

One evening after work, McKinley saw some beautiful flowers on the side of the road. Yes, he had gotten out to pick them. They were lilies and he wanted to give them to wife to let her know how much he loved her and appreciated her. When he made it home and walked in the door, Minnie was cooking dinner on their new cast- iron stove in the kitchen. To keep it going, you had to keep adding fresh wood. It was what you would call a potbelly stove. It also kept the house warm. You would have to set it on bricks so that it wouldn't burn through the floor and catch the house on fire. McKinley always walked up to his wife and kissed her on her neck when he got home from work. Now, McKinley was holding the flowers in his hand, behind his back. He pulled them out and said to her, "Momma, these are for you!"

Minnie looked very pleasantly surprised and said to her husband, "Thank you, thank you, honey!" Minnie said to her husband, "I have some news for the both of us."

"Okay! Well, let me wash up first. Then we can talk about it."

Minnie said, "Okay."

There wasn't any running water in the house. McKinley went out to the well and put some water in a pot and then on the stove so he could have some hot water to clean himself up for dinner and for the night. Now, all cleaned up, McKinley sat down at the dinner table, holding his baby, talking to her, playing with her. Baby Christine would just smile at her daddy! "Now, Minnie, what was it that you wanted to tell me?"

Minnie didn't say anything right away. Then she said, "Hold on a minute. Let me make your plate." Minnie placed her husband's plate in front of him and then sat down with her plate as well.

McKinley said, "Well? Well? What's going on?"

Minnie said, "I will tell you just as soon as you give God the grace and the glory for what we have. Also, for the food that we are about to eat."

"You're right," said McKinley. "Father God, I want to first of all say thank you for allowing me and my family to wake up this morning! Thank you, Lord, for giving us the opportunity to sit down together and break bread with each other. Thank you for providing a way for us, keeping me with a job, also keeping us with a house of worship. Thank you, Lord, in your son Jesus' holy name, Amen!" McKinley then lifted his head and immediately looked over at his wife. "What is wrong?"

Minnie looked at McKinley, saying to him, "We are pregnant!"

McKinley said, "This is wonderful! I always wanted more than one child. I grew up without any sisters or brothers. Now our daughter will have a sister or a brother! This is great news."

Then Minnie said to McKinley, "You wanted to share some news with me."   "Well, it's just that I want to go to Memphis, Tennessee. I was telling you that I wanted to find my birth father." Minnie didn't say anything about how she felt about McKinley wanting to go chase a man who clearly didn't give a damn about him.   Because if he did, he would have come to see the son that he had outside his marriage.   Yet, Minnie would stand behind him and give him her love and support. McKinley would talk about this for the next seven months.

It was time for the birth of the new baby!   Baby Christine had just turned one year old. On November 1, 1928, Minnie gave birth to another baby girl. "We will name her Beatrice Newton," said McKinley. He was beaming with so much joy as he enjoyed and loved his girls and his wife.

The following year, yes, Minnie was pregnant again. McKinley and Minnie's first son arrived in October 1929. He was named Robert Newton. The babies just kept on coming. It was now 1931, and another little girl was born. She was named Martha after McKinley's mother. Yes, the babies were still coming. The year was 1933, another son. He was named McKinley Newton. In 1935, another little girl.   Her name was Annie Newton. The next year, 1936, another little girl. Her name was Rosetta Newton. Yes, early in the next year, 1937, another little girl named Elizabeth Newton arrived. Minnie and McKinley now had eight children! The house was busy and chaotic, but Minnie did her best to keep things together. Minnie didn't have much room or time for herself. The only time Minnie had to herself was when she attended church. When McKinley and Minnie got to church, the congregation would pitch in to help give them some relief. It was some comfort and peace of mind for Minnie.

McKinley, however, made sure to attend every meeting he could to get away from the family. Sunday School meeting! Deacon board meeting! It was to the point that he was never home for dinner on time. Also, every time Minnie would look around, there was Hattie in McKinley's face, smiling and giggling.

Now Minnie's dad, Walter, had seen that his daughter wasn't happy. So, one Sunday when church was over, her dad said to her, "I will be by. I have a surprise for you." That put a smile on Minnie's face! Minnie's mom, Beatrice, had tried to help by taking their son Robert to live with her. Robert had lived with his grandmother for the past six years. On this particular Sunday, when church was over, the congregation was all outside in the parking lot saying their goodbyes until they would meet again. McKinley drove Minnie and the children home. As they pulled up to the house, McKinley barely helped his wife and children into the house before he left for another church event. He got back into his truck and made his way down the road, leaving Minnie, with a sense of disbelief, standing there watching his truck disappear into the dust. Now Minnie never would question what her husband would do up until this point of their marriage. About five minutes later, Minnie could hear someone pulling up in front of their house. It was her father, Walter Marley. Minnie walked out onto the porch and greeted her dad, saying to him, "Hi, Daddy."

Now, answering his little girl, "HI, SWEETIE."

"Daddy, what is that you have with you?"

"Well, first of all, this is the surprise I was telling you about." Walter had given Minnie a horse! He had also given his daughter a rifle. "Now, I know that you don't drive yet, but you still need to be able to get around. Also, I want you to practice shooting your rifle. You never know how and when you might have to defend yourself from an animal or even an unruly person. I see that you have been left to take care of these children most of the time by yourself."

"You're right, Dad!" Minnie had cooked dinner and asked her dad to join them.

Walter Marley said, "Yes, I would love to stay." He played with his grandkids. Also, he made mention of the fact that the last baby Minnie had took after his side of the family--expressing that Elizabeth looked like a white baby! Minnie said to her dad, "All my children look the same."

The evening was fast approaching. Walter was now saying his goodbyes, also saying to his daughter, "Hmm, I see your husband is not home yet." Minnie ignored this statement and proceeded to tell her dad good-night and thank him for her new horse and rifle. Now, later on that night, after the children were all asleep, McKinley finally walked through the door.

With only two bedrooms in the house, the older children slept in one bedroom. Three beds in the room with the children, two or three kids to a bed. The older girls were close, and one child, Robert, lived with Minnie's mother. McKinley said to Minnie, "Where is my dinner?" Minnie pretended that she didn't hear him. McKinley, in a very loud and very unpleasant tone of voice yelled, "Woman, get up and get my dinner!" waking up everyone. Minnie got up and did what she was asked to do. After attending to her husband's demands, Minnie went to comfort her children, to ease their fear of their dad's behavior. When the children were all back to sleep, Minnie also made her way to bed after a very long and exhausting day.

Meanwhile, over at her mother's house, her son Robert lived. He was eight years old at the time. Robert never really understood why he was separated from the other children. There was really no explanation given as to why he lived with his grandmother, other than the fact that she thought she was helping out. This left young Robert with so many questions.

The only time Robert saw his dad was when he would pick him up to work with him in the field picking cotton. Well, on one particular Monday, McKinley picked Robert up for work. He and his dad made it to their work site, where everyone was busy doing their job. Then, about 30 minutes after arriving at work, Robert could see his dad getting in his truck with the woman who went to the church they all attended. Yes, it was Hattie! The both of them were gone for most of the morning and no one knew where they were. Young Robert did not know what was going on. What were they doing?

Robert would hear the other people talking and laughing about their whereabouts. Also, when it was time to be paid, McKinley would take the money that Robert had worked so hard for. Now, this only made young Robert bitter, although he just kept on working.

Meanwhile, while Robert was working in the fields, McKinley would ride off with Hattie to a nice, secluded place in the woods. McKinley would pull his truck over. Hattie would not be able to keep her hands to herself. Now rubbing her hand all up and down McKinley's leg, you could see through McKinley's pants that his penis had a very hard erection. Barely putting the truck in park, he would jump out of the truck and walk around to the passenger side. McKinley would take off his shirt and open up the door. Hattie had already taken off her panties and spread her legs wide open. McKinley would drop his pants. Taking his finger and placing it inside of her vagina, Hattie would moan and then sigh with pleasure. She would slide to the end of the seat with one leg on the door of the truck and the other leg on McKinley's shoulder. He would lean in and start to quiver, moving his finger in and out of her vagina in a slow but steady motion. Hattie was expressing how she enjoyed McKinley's touch. Hattie told McKinley that she was ready for him to put his penis inside of her. So, he did just that, moving his body back and forth with uncontrollable motion love. This went on for hours until the both of them would have an orgasm or climax. After they were done, they would clean themselves up and then head back to the work site as if they had been working all day! Hattie would come back with her hair all over the place. It only gave the other workers more ammunition to use against them.

Later on that day, when it was time to go home, Robert would get in the truck with his dad and Hattie. Robert paid close attention to his dad's actions. He would see McKinley looking over at Hattie and giving her a real big smile, telling her to have a good night. "I will see you later on at Bible Study," McKinley said to her.

Now, on the way to drop Robert off at his grandmother's house, Robert asked his father, "Dad, where do you go off to with that Miss Hattie?" McKinley's mind was somewhere else. "Dad! Dad!"

"What, son?"

"Where do you and Miss Hattie go off to in the morning when we get to work?"

McKinley yelled at his son, "Nowhere. We work in another part of the field. Miss Hattie was just being nice, and it's none of your business. Let me tell you something: You don't question me about what I do! I am a man. You are a boy. You are my son, and you do as I tell you. Do you understand me?"

Robert said to his dad, "Yes!" The rest of the ride was quiet as Robert grew more and more bitter toward his dad.

As they pulled up to his grandmother's house, Robert said in a very low voice, "Bye."

McKinley said, "I will see you bright and early tomorrow!" Before he pulled off, he could see Miz Beatrice Draper and Walter Marley on the porch just chilling. "Hey, how are you both doing?"

"Well, we are good!"

McKinley said, "Well, that is good to hear," before he drove off down the road. Robert walked up the stairs with his head hung down. His grandma told him that his dinner was ready and he should go wash up.

"I will be in there in a few minutes."

His grandma said to him, "Why the sad face?" Robert said nothing. So, his grandma said, "Your dinner is ready, go wash up."

"I will be in there in a few minutes." Robert's grandfather and grandmother stayed on the porch talking for a few minutes before going in the house. Robert was done washing up and he sat down at the kitchen table with his grandma and granddad. Knowing how hungry Robert must be, his grandma placed his dinner in front of him. His grandparents looked at each other, and then Walter asked, "Son, what is wrong? Why are you looking so sad?"

Robert just looked and then said to them, "Nothing is wrong." For about five minutes it was quiet. Then Robert said with tears in his eyes, "My dad just makes me sick!"

His grandma said to him, "Baby, what do you mean? Why would you say that about your dad?"

Robert said, "Well, it's true. All he does is drop me off at work, then takes that lady Hattie somewhere and they are gone all day. Then, when it's time to get paid, he takes my money I work for. Grandma, now that is not right."

Beatrice and Walter said to their grandson, "Are you sure about this?"

"Yes, I'm sure."

His grandparents looked at each other. His grandma said to him, "Sweetie, finish up your dinner. I will be on the porch talking to your granddad." Beatrice and Walter went outside and had a very deep discussion about what their grandson had shared with them. Miz Beatrice was saying to Walter, "You know we should tell Minnie about what is going on!"

Walter answered, "Now, now, now! Even though I don't like what is going on, it is none of our business. Besides, we didn't see any of this with our own eyes." Beatrice said, "No, we didn't, but that doesn't mean it didn't happen. Besides, it makes me downright angry." After a few minutes of their conversation, Robert walked out onto the porch to inform his grandma that he was done eating. She said, "Okay, sweetie, come sit with us and relax." By now it was getting dark outside, and his grandma started to sing. Then they would talk some more. Then it would get so quiet you could hear the crickets in the yard. The sky was deep blue and clear. Bugs were flying around and started to become a nuisance, so his grandma took out the kerosene lantern which would keep the bugs to a minimum while also shedding some light and brightening up the area. Without the lantern, it was so dark, you couldn't see your hand in front of your face.

Robert liked to lie back and talk endlessly to his grandparents. He was so very comfortable telling then anything and everything. He was also very fond of the way his granddad told stories that could captivate everyone. As the night drew on, his grandma would remind Robert that he needed his rest and he should get ready for bed. "Now, you know your dad will be here bright and early." Robert would go to bed as his grandma blew out the light.

The sun had started to rise. You could hear the rooster crow cock-a-doodle- doo. The morning air was so special. The morning dew. Robert's grandma was up and would always make sure her husband and grandson had a healthy and hearty breakfast. Miz Beatrice would also make sure that the both of them would enjoy a good lunch as well. Walter would make his way to work. He had a new position at the sheriff's office. It was said that he was in charge of keeping the Black people in order in the community where he lived. Now Grandma was kissing Walter goodbye for the day and watching Robert sit on the porch waiting on his dad to drive up. Robert couldn't keep his mind from wondering why was he separated from his mom and his siblings.

Miz Beatrice stood in the doorway making sure that her grandson was safely secured with his dad. McKinley pulled up then and said good morning to Miz Beatrice. In a little voice she responded, "Good morning, McKinley."

Robert said goodbye to his grandma. "I will see you soon," he said as he closed the door to his dad's truck. Now McKinley drove off heading to work, and Miz Beatrice watched the truck disappear from her site. Not feeling her best, she went back into the house and laid on her bed to rest until later.

After putting in a full day's work, McKinley arrived at Walter and Beatrice's house to drop off his son, but that's when he noticed something peculiar about this day. Granddad was home early. All of his brothers-in-law were there as well. So, McKinley got out of the truck with his son. As the both of them were walking up the stairs, Johnny Marley walked out the door to sit in a chair on the porch. McKinley said hello and then asked Johnny whether everything was all right. Johnny put his head down and then said, "No."

Robert rushed in the door at this point. He ran to where his grandmother was laying in her bed lifeless. Robert started to cry. He fell to the side of her bed and placed her cold hand on his face, saying, "No! No! Grandma."

His granddad said, "Son, come on, let's go for a walk."

Robert said, "I can't leave her now." Robert sat there next to his grandma for hours talking to her and brushing her hair with his hand. McKinley had gone home to get his wife, Minnie, to let her know what had happened to her mother. Robert was still at her bedside when his mother walked through the bedroom door.

Minnie said to her dad, "What happened?" She wanted to hear it from her dad.

"I came home, like I would always do to check on your mom. I could see that it was quiet. As I was getting out of my truck, I called out her name. 'Beatrice!' She would normally answer me. I thought it was strange when she didn't. It was so surreal. I walked into our bedroom. I took a deep breath and was relieved to see her lying there asleep. I got in the bed to put my arms around her, and that's when I realized that my sweetie was lifeless. I held her and I began to cry. My heart is shattered." Minnie was sitting on the side of the bed and leaned in to kiss her mother. She also started to cry. Now Walter went over to console his daughter.

The word was out now about the passing of Miz Beatrice. There was a knock at the door. Soon the house was crowded with family coming to see if it was true about the death of Miz Beatrice. Now at the door was the pastor of their church. Yes, it was Pastor White. One of Walter's sons had answered the door. "Please come on in."

Pastor White said, "The news travels real fast. I'm so sorry for your loss. I come to pray over her." Walter escorted the pastor into the bedroom to where Miz Beatrice's body was lying. Robert and Minnie were still in the room with her body. Pastor White said again, "I'm so sorry for your momma." Miz Minnie thanked him. "Let us pray now." Pastor White said.

"Father God, we have come here humble as we can. Lord, you have called home our beloved sister, Mrs. Beatrice Draper. Yes, we loved her, yet you needed her more. Father God, she is going to be missed. Please place your arms around her children, and also her grandchildren. Lord, place your arms around her husband. Give this family the strength to comfort them in their time of need. In Jesus' name we pray, Amen."

It was only a few minutes later when there was another knock at the door. Two men standing there. You couldn't really see their faces because it was dark. You could see their shadows on the porch. One of the sons, Othea, had opened up the door. The two men said, "We were called here to pick up someone that had passed. We are from the William H. Jefferson Funeral Home. Our family business has been around since 1894." Now standing in the doorway was Othea inviting them in and showing them to his mother's bedroom. The pastor and Minnie and also her son Robert were still in the room. Everyone knew why the two men were there.

Robert had to have one last moment with his grandma before they took her away. Robert fell to his knees and started to cry, "Please, Grandma, please open up your eyes." His granddad could hear him from the other room.

Walter walked in and put his arms around his grandson saying, "It's going to be all right," as he walked Robert outside to sit on the back of his truck. He said, "Son, I know how much you loved your grandma. Guess what, she also loved you with her whole heart. There is nothing that she would not do for you. Son, always keep your grandma tucked away in your heart."

Robert looked at his granddad. Then he asked, "Now what is gong to happen to me? Where will I live? Where will I go?"

His granddad looked at his grandson with tears in his eyes. "Son, you can live here with me. We can make it together."

The men from the funeral home were bringing Miz Beatrice out of the house. They placed her in the hearse. The men walked over to Walter Marley and handed him clipboard with a piece of paper to sign to allow them to receive the responsibility to arrange her funeral. Walter signed the paper, and the men proceeded down the road as everyone gathered to watch Miz Beatrice leave. The night was very, so very quiet. One by one everyone made their way to their vehicles.

Hugging all of his children goodnight before they went home, Walter then sat with Robert on the porch, Walter rocking in his wooden chair. "I know that you are hungry. You need your rest. You can go with me tomorrow." Robert got up and headed for the door and ran over and gave his granddad the biggest hug. Walter hugged him back as he said to his grandson, "We will be all right."

The next morning Robert was up bright and early in the kitchen trying to make his granddad some breakfast and coffee. Walter was lying in the bed that he and his wife had shared. He was having a very hard time comprehending what had happened. He pulled himself together before he made his way into the kitchen. When he walked into the kitchen, he said to Robert, "Son, what are you doing?"

Oh, Granddad, I am making you something to eat. You know we need to be strong. Granddad, I'm just looking out for you!"

"Thank you, son."

Selvie walked into the house, talking in a very loud voice. "Hey, Dad! Hey, Bob! Good morning! Dad, I came by to see if I could help you with anything."

Walter said to his son, "Well, we're on our way down to the funeral home to make arrangements. If you like, you can go with us."

Selvie and Robert formed a closer bond from this point on. It was like Robert was Selvie's little brother rather than his nephew. Now, you would think that Robert would go to stay with his mom and dad. But the subject just never came up! Besides, Robert was just a little boy. He was only eight years old and had to stay close to his granddad and also his uncle Selvie.

The three of them made their way to the funeral home and went inside to handle the arrangements. About an hour later, they were done. "The funeral will be held at Good Hope Missionary Baptist Church," Mr. Walter Marley said to his son and grandson. "Since we are already here, we need to get a few things from the market," he said. The market was close to the area that they were in, downtown Vicksburg, Mississippi.

Now Selvie was having a conversation with his dad about what was going on in his life. "So, Dad, I don't know how to tell you this. I'm going to be a dad! My wife, Annie May Shelton, is having our baby."

"Now, son, tell me how this will work. I thought you were with that lady named Stella that works at the juke joint."

"Oh, yeah! I'm still with her too."

"Son! How and where did you get this behavior from?"

"Dad, I got it from you! I have watched you do our mother like that. Man! Don't think because we haven't said anything to you that we don't know about the many women that you have scattered over the state of Mississippi. Oh, Dad! I know that when you went to Yazoo, the people there would think that you were a white man. Dad, I also know that we have a half-sister that also lives in Yazoo. So please, Dad, don't."

"Now, son, first of all, how do you know about this? Who told you about my life?"

"My mom did! Dad, I could see the pain that it caused her. I watched my mom when you were not around trying to explain your absence. We never questioned you or our mom."

"Selvie, I'm just trying to save you from the mess that I had to endure. Son, I know that it wasn't right. I need you to know that I love your mother with everything. I can't explain the drive of being with the other women and having children with them too. I guess it felt so good to being treated so different. It was like day and night. Son, when I came to these towns Edward and Vicksburg, I was treated like a Black man. When I went to Yazoo, I was treated like a white man. I was treated with so much privilege, son, that I just got caught up in my own selfish ways. I know this may not come out of my mouth the right way, but please hear me. Your momma was my everything. I'm lost now without her in my life. Please forgive me for my actions."

Selvie said to his dad, "I understand, Dad. I know how you feel. I like the attention that I get from Stella, but I have a big responsibility to my wife, Annie. Now I have to make a choice in my life. I have a child on the way! Stella thinks it's just me and her. I need to tell her the truth."

"Son, I will leave that up to you. Right now I can only think about making it through this funeral."

"You're right, Dad. That is what is on my mind as well." Walter leaned over and give his son a big hug.

It was the morning of the funeral. Good Hope Baptist Church. The whole congregation came out to assist the Marley family in saying goodbye to their beloved sister and mother, Mrs. Beatrice Draper. Being here to lay Miz Beatrice to rest. The pastor welcomed the funeral home staff into the church to bring in the casket to be placed at the altar. The service would start at 11:00 AM. Now family after family entered the church one by one, coming up to the casket to view her body. Sitting right in front of the casket, her husband, Walter Marley. Then his baby girl, Minnie, and McKinley. Walter's four sons: Johnny, Othea, Selvie, Moody. What a legacy she leaves behind. Pastor White delivered a wonderful home-going celebration. There was a joyful choir singing so strong and loud you could feel the presence of the Holy Ghost!

As the service came to an end, the pastor led the family out of the church, walking behind the casket and reciting Psalm 23: "The Lord is my shepherd; I shall not want. He maketh me to lie down in green pastures: He leadeth me beside the still waters. He restoreth my soul; He leadeth me in the path of righteousness for his name's sake. Yea, though I walk through the valley of the shadow of death, I will fear no evil: for thou art with me; thy rod and thy staff they comfort me. Thou preparest a table before me in the presence of mine enemies: thou anointest my head with oil, my cup runneth over. Surely goodness and mercy shall follow me all the days of my life; and I will dwell in the house of the Lord forever. Amen.

Everyone was outside greeting the family to give hugs and words of encouragement, also words of condolences. Tearful hugs, knowing that Miz Beatrice would be missed. Then it was time to lay Miz Beatrice to rest at the cemetery. The family piled into their own vehicles following the hearse. Standing at the hearse at the cemetery were her four sons. It was only fitting for them to carry her to her final resting place. As everyone was gathering for prayer, Pastor White said his last words. "Ashes to ashes, dust to dust."

Then everyone was making their way back to their cars. Yet Walter Marley sat at his wife's side, not wanting to leave. He stayed there for hours. It was so painful for him. Selvie and Robert came back to see if he was still at Miz Beatrice's grave site. Yes, he was. Young Robert walked up to his granddad saying,

"Granddad, it's time to go home," holding his hand as they walked to his truck, and then making their way home.

With the recent death of his wife, Walter started drinking more frequently. He was drinking morning and night. On one particular day a few months after his wife's death, Mr. Walter Marley was very concerned for his daughter. He wanted to know how she was doing. He was aware that she had her hands full with having eight children. The youngest three were only a year apart and were all wearing diapers. The baby was only six months old. Walter was knocking at his daughter's front door,   yelling out loud, "Is anyone home?"

Minnie yelled out from the back yard, "Daddy, I'm in the back."

"Oh, there you are."

"Hi, Dad, I'm washing and hanging up diapers." Now the children had seen their grand dad! They were jumping up and down with so much joy and excitement, grabbing onto his legs. He was very happy to see them as well.

The older children were asking their granddad if they could please go get some ice cream. "Please! Please!"

"Well, you will have to ask your mother."

So the children said at the same time, "Please, Mom, please, can we go?"   Miz Minnie said, "Yes. Now, don't stay gone too long." The youngest children stayed with their mom. Robert had stayed back at his granddad's house. Now off they went into town. The ride was fun and fast. Lots of laughing and singing. The children were telling their granddad what was going on in their little lives. The oldest three girls and little McKinley-- he was only five years old. The ice cream parlor is where the Black people would go without having any incidents.   Granddad had walked the children up to the window, saying without thinking, "Children, is that your dad over at the market?"

The girls yelled, "Hi, Daddy!" Mckinley Sr. waved to his children and finally made his way across the street, giving his children real big hugs.

His son asked, "Dad, what are you doing with Miss Hattie?"

"Well, son, I was just giving Miss Hattie a ride to the market."

"Daddy, what is that you have in your hand?"

"Oh, this? It's just some good old sugar cane. So, I have to make sure I give Miss Hattie a ride home. I will see you guys soon."

"Okay, Daddy!"

McKinley Sr.'s father-in-law said to him, "I will see you soon." The children had finished up their ice cream. Granddad said to the children, "It's time to make our way home."

All talking at the same time, "Please, Granddad, can we have another ice cream cone?"

"No, I think that is enough. You don't want to spoil your dinner."

"Okay, thank you for the ice cream." Everyone piled into the truck. The children were very hyper, singing their songs, "This Little Light of Mine, I'm Going to Let it Shine," over and over again. Now, after riding for 20 minutes, they were back at their home. The girls got out of the truck and made their way into the house. They went to their bedroom with sad faces and their heads held down. McKinley Jr. (nicknamed Mack) said to his mother, "Mom I saw dad with Miz Hattie, and Dad had a whole heap of sugar cane. I can't wait until Daddy gets home. Then all the sugar cane will be mine.

Now Miz Minnie wasn't very pleased with the news her son had just shared with her. Minnie asked her dad, "Is this true?"

Her dad answered, "Now you know that I don't like getting in nobody's business, but, sweetie, yes, it is true. Meanwhile, you could see the hurt on his daughter's face and in her eyes which were full of tears. At this point, she was very angry! Trying to hold things together, Minnie started to prepare dinner for the children. The older girls did their part in helping out their mother. After dinner was over with, Minnie, still not herself, walked out onto the porch, then looked around before she sat down. Her dad was still there as well.   He had come out the door right behind her. It was getting well into the night and still no sign of McKinley. Four hours had gone by since he was last seen. Minnie started to get angry all over again!   "Dad, I need you to watch the children for me. I will be back as soon as I can.   Her dad said, "Yes, I will watch the children. I will have the girls help me if I need them." Minnie went into the house and into her bedroom, thumbing through her clothes, trying to decide what she wanted to wear. She found a sweater and pulled it over her head. Then she pulled some pants on and put her hair back up into a ponytail. Then she went to her closet and got her rifle. She put the rifle over her shoulder. Minnie was very much determined as she walked outside right past her dad. He asked Minnie, "Where are you going?" But then he said, "Oh, never mind."   Minnie untied her horse. As she walked her horse to the front of the house, she called out, "Hey, Dad, could you help me saddle up my horse please? Her dad put on the saddle as Minnie held the horse still. Then he held the horse so she would be able to get on it. Minnie turned to her dad and said, "I will see you soon," as she galloped off into the night. The night sky was a royal blue. The stars in the sky shone oh so bright. You could hear the owl in the back yard hooting Whoo, whoo.

Now Minnie rode her horse with the full moon beaming on her path. Making her way to her destination, she arrived right in front of Miss Hattie's house. Minnie walked her horse over to a nearby tree and tied him up. She looked behind the house and saw her husband's truck hiding in the back yard. She walked up to the front of the house, taking her rifle off her back. Minnie cocked her rifle and pointed it to the sky. Minnie shot--bang! Soon, she could see someone peek out of the window. She could also hear someone moving about inside the house. The sound of the gunshot had made the horse afraid and upset. Minnie said real loud, "McKinley, I know you can hear me! I know that your ass is up in this house." She shot her rifle again, saying, "McKinley you had better come out of there now, NOW!

Nobody would budge, though, so Minnie started to walk toward the front door. Something came over her, however, that stopped her in her tracks. Minnie had thought about her children and wondered what it would do to them if she went inside and killed their dad. Or, what if she were to get hurt? Besides, Minnie also loved her husband with everything that she had in her. So, speaking in a real loud voice, "McKinley! I tell you what--I'm going to leave here. I'm going to give you one chance. You had better get your ass home before I get there." Minnie got herself together, climbed on her horse, and galloped off into the night.

McKinley and Hattie walked outside onto the porch. McKinley told Hattie, "I have to go." Without any hesitation, moving real fast, McKinley got into his truck and drove off like a lightning bolt, making his way home. When he arrived, he could see his father-in-law's truck parked in front of his house. McKinley sat in his truck for a moment, trying to gather his thoughts. Talking to himself, saying, "Here goes," he opened up the door of his truck. Walking up the stairs and into the house.

His father-in-law spoke first. Then McKinley said, "Hey, Dad." He asked where his wife was. Walter said she had some business to take care of and wouldn't be gone too long. McKinley replied, "Okay." Before he could finish his sentence, the door opened. It was Minnie.

She looked at her dad and said, "Thank you for watching the children."

He said "Oh, sweetie, no problem. I really had a great time with them all.   It's time for me to go home now."

Minnie said, "I love you, Dad."

He said, "I love you, too," as he walked out of the door. McKinley tried to talk to his wife. Minnie looked at McKinley and said nothing. She ignored him as she put away her rifle. Minnie went into the other room and got herself ready for bed. McKinley went to bed soon afterwards, and while lying in bed, he was still trying to talk to his wife. Minnie still would not talk to him. Then the both of them went fast to sleep!

For the next few months, life for everyone was very routine. One sunny day, Minnie was up as usual, cooking breakfast for her husband and her children, when there was a knock at the door. It was Minnie's dad. "Good morning, everyone!"   You could see that Mr. Walter Marley was having a very hard time coping with the loss of his wife. He was rambling on about how much he missed his wife, Miz Beatrice. Not making any sense with his conversation.

Now his daughter said, "Dad, I'm going to make you something to eat."

Walter gave her this long look and answered real slow, "Okay. Thank you."   McKinley grabbed his hat and gave his wife a big kiss. "I will see you right after work." Minnie said okay as McKinley walked out the door.

Minnie and her dad sat down at the kitchen table. Both of them eating when Mr. Walter said to his daughter, "I'm going into town. I want to take the baby into my job to show her off, yes! Now everyone would see that my baby looks white. Oh I know that she's Black. But nobody has to know."

Minnie looked at her dad with a look of disbelief. Then she answered him, "Dad, no, you can't take my baby into town. You really need to go home and get yourself cleaned up and get some rest."

Walter answered, "Yeah, yeah, yeah." But he sat there for another two hours, talking and falling off to sleep. Then, all of a sudden, he popped up and said he had to go to work. He walked over to his daughter and gave her a big hug and kiss, something that he normally didn't do. He said to Minnie, "Baby, I love you," as he walked out the door and climbed into his truck. Still a little confused, he was now driving into town and making his way to work. Finally, he arrived at work.

There were some joyriders behind Walter who had not been able to pass him on the road. Now Walter got out of his truck, upset with the other drivers and yelling at them. The other drivers yelled back, and Walter heard them saying, "You nigger lover." One driver was so upset with Walter that he turned his truck around and then charged at him, hitting him with his truck so hard that Walter flew into the air. Sadly, Mr. Walter Marley succumbed to the fall from the impact and lay on the ground lifeless, only to be run over again before someone recognized him.

This happened right outside the sheriff's office. The sheriff came to make a report, trying to gather information on what had happened and who to contact as the next of kin. The sheriff called the local funeral home for the white people, not even thinking all of this time that Mr. Walter Marley was in fact a Black man. The sheriff looked at the contact information and sent out one of his deputies to inform the next of kin, which was Minnie Newton. The deputy arrived at Minnie's house, got out of his vehicle, and walked up the stairs to the front door. He began knocking. Minnie looked out of the window. Minnie opened up the door and the deputy said to her, "Are you Minnie Marley Newton?"

"Yes, I am."

The deputy said, "Well, I'm sorry to inform you that Mr. Walter Marley was unfortunately killed this morning around 11:00 AM. He was run over by a truck, and before we could get there, he was run over again. I'm so sorry for your loss. He told her the name of the funeral home Walter had been taken to. Miz Minnie was taken aback by this news that was given to her. Then she asked the older children, the three older girls, to keep an eye on the younger children. Minnie went into her bedroom where she cried, in so much pain from the information that she had taken in. Lying there in her bed, resting.

Now a few hours had passed and McKinley arrived home. He made sure never to never be late coming home again. He noticed that it was very quiet. Normally Minnie would be cooking dinner or be done cooking. McKinley was greeted by one of his oldest daughters, Beatrice, who was named after her grandmother. "Hi, Dad," she said in her very quiet voice.

McKinley said, "Good evening. Where is your mother?"

"Mom is lying down in her bedroom."

McKinley hung up his hat that he had in his hand and then proceeded to walk into their bedroom. He called out Minnie's name as he sat on the side of the bed next to his wife. He said, "Momma what's the matter?" Minnie looked at her husband with her eyes full of tears. She explained to him about the death of her dad. He started to cry as well. McKinley put his arms around Minnie as the both of them wept. McKinley held his wife so tight.

Now as they calmed each other down, Minnie gave her husband the information the sheriff's deputy had given her. "This is where you can go to pick up Dad's body."

McKinley said to Minnie, "Yes, first thing in the morning."

"Oh, before I forget," said Minnie, "go over to the house and get Robert. He is there all by himself. Now we can't have that. I also want you to tell him that his granddad was killed."

McKinley said, "Yes, I will take care of everything. I will also let your brothers know as well." McKinley went over to where their son was at the house where his in-laws lived. He got out of his truck and walked up on the porch. The door was open and he could see his son Robert sitting at the kitchen table. McKinley stood on the porch, not knowing how he was going to be able to tell his son that his granddad had been killed! He took a deep breath. Then he exhaled as he knocked on the door, saying out loud, "Hey, son!

Robert answered him saying, "Hi," as he looked up at his dad.

Robert knew that something was wrong because his dad never came over other than to pick him up for work. "Well, son, I came over to pick you up. There was an incident with your grandfather."

Robert was still sitting there looking up at his dad whose eyes started to well up with tears. Robert became very nervous and asked, "What is wrong?"

"Well, son, your granddad was killed. He was run over with a truck, and as his body lay in the road, he was run over again."

Robert jumped up and ran to his room. He was crying and saying out loud, "NO! NO! I don't want to go with you!"

McKinley sat down at the table, trying to understand his son's feelings. Taking himself some deep breaths. Then he went into the room that Robert had just gone into and sat down on the bed. "Now, son, I know that I haven't been here for you. I'm trying to be here for you now. I can't allow you to stay here. You know that you're still a child." Robert didn't say anything. He gathered up a few things   Then both of them got into the truck and made their way back to the house where Robert's siblings and his mom were. McKinley walked into the house and proceeded to the kitchen, asking Robert if he was hungry. Robert said he was. Then his dad made him something to eat. The both of them started talking. McKinley was saying that he needed to go to town the next day and get the body of Mr. Walter Marley. Robert asked if he could go along. His dad said, "Yes you can go with me, but in the meantime, you need to get ready for bed. You will sleep in this room. Robert walked into the other bedroom in the house. He could see that everyone was asleep. All of his seven siblings were in their beds. There were three beds in this room, and every bed was full. There was no place for Robert to sleep. So, he took his blanket to the living room and slept on the floor. The night was calm and peaceful.

The next morning Minnie was up cooking breakfast for everyone. You could hear one by one all eight of the children making so much noise about the house. Now everyone getting their meal in getting ready to go about their day. McKinley Sr. talked with all of his children, and then he grabbed his hat and kissed his wife as he walked out of the door. Robert was walking right behind him. McKinley sat inside his truck with his son Robert, checking over the information about where he needed to go to pick up the body of his deceased father-in-law. "Well, son, it looks like we need to go to Riles Funeral Home."

"Okay, Dad!" On the way to the funeral home, McKinley Sr. was telling his son Robert all that he would expect out of him. Robert listened to his father but wasn't very happy with what he was saying. Robert felt that his dad was putting all of his responsibilities on him. Now remember, it was the summer of 1938 and Robert was only eight years old and would be nine by the end of that year. They finally made it to their destination, both father and son standing in front of Riles Funeral Home. Both of them were wearing hats, and as they entered this funeral home, they proceeded to take their hats off. McKinley had taken only a few steps before he was cut off by the funeral director. Now he was just standing there with his son. The director was Caucasian. McKinley said, "Good morning, sir."

The director said, "If you have any product or a load, it should be taken in the back door. We don't let niggers come to our front door."

McKinley said, "Oh no, sir. I'm here with some information. I believe that you may have my father-in-law here. It seems that he was taken to the wrong place." "Well, let me get you straight. You have come to the wrong place. I'm going to say this again. We don't serve niggers in our funeral home, so you have the wrong place." Then, to make matters worse, he made them go out the service door now for fear they would hurt his business.

McKinley Sr. and his son made their way back to the truck. The two of them sat there with this feeling of being inadequate. Robert looked at his dad, asking him, "What are you going to do now?"

"I'm not sure." But then McKinley had this light bulb moment that went off in his head. So he turned his truck in another direction. McKinley pulled up in front of the bank that was in town. McKinley said, "Son, come with me." They got out of the truck and walked into the bank, and McKinley asked the receptionist if he could see Mr. Will Montgomery. After being gone for a few minutes, the receptionist returned to let him know that Mr. Montgomery would be right with him as soon as he finished up with another customer. McKinley said real kindly, "Thank you."

Fifteen minutes went by before Mr. Will Montgomery walked up to McKinley. He extended his hand to give a very firm handshake. "Good afternoon, how have you been? How is the family?"

"We are just fine."

Mr. Montgomery asked, "Now, what can I do for you?"

"Well, sir, I have a problem. I was wondering if you could help me. You see, it's about my father-in-law. He was in this terrible accident. He was hit by a vehicle where he was killed. He was left on the road dead."

"Oh my! I'm so sorry to hear this."

"Yes, thank you for being so caring. My problem is that the authorities have taken his body to a funeral home where Negroes are not allowed. My father-in-law is in fact a Negro man. Where they have taken his body, they believe that he is a Caucasian man. So, when I tried to retrieve his body from the funeral home, the funeral director wouldn't even try to hear what I had to say. He was more concerned with the color of my skin. So this is my predicament. Please, if you would, go over there and see if Riles Funeral Home would drop his body off at the right place."

Mr. Montgomery said to McKinley, "I sure will. I get off my job around 5:00 PM, and then I will go right over there and handle this situation." McKinley gave him all the information that was needed. Upon leaving, McKinley thanked him for his help.

Now McKinley said to his son, "Mr. Montgomery is a righteous man of God." They got back in the truck and drove down the road, making their way back to the house. Everywhere McKinley had stopped, people were giving him and his wife, Minnie, their sincere condolences. Yes, Walter had been well loved.

The one person that was most deeply affected by Walter's death was Robert Newton. Even though he was his grandson, the only two people that he felt loved him unconditionally were now gone. It was like he had lost his parents. Everyone was gathered that day at McKinley and Minnie's house trying to make the proper arrangements for Walter Marley's funeral. The host of family and friends was so overwhelming for Robert. He felt like he didn't fit in.

Robert's uncle Selvie was sitting back and looking at his nephew, trying to show him that he cared. Selvie Marley from here on out would take on his dad's name. Everyone would call him Marley or Uncle Marley. Now he went up to Robert and said, "Are you okay?"

Robert started to cry and said, "No, I'm not."

"Well, son, you will be okay. You know, when this is all over with, I will make sure to come over and take you fishing."

Robert said, "Yes, I would like that," as the family shared stories of Walter Marley's life, laughing and crying about the life he lived, well into the night.

One week has gone by, and all of the arrangements had been made. The parking lot at the church was full. Everybody was making their way inside the church to pay their respects to Mr. Walter Marley. The family was sitting all together. It was a very hard thing to go through. His daughter, Minnie, and her husband,

McKinley, his four sons and their wives. Selvie's wife Annie was with child about seven months along. Johnny and his wife, and Cleotha and his wife. His nickname was Othea. Then there was Moody and his wife. Yes, all of Walter's brothers has also come to pay their respects to their brother. Yes, there was Mr. Will Marley. Then there was Mr. Masey Marley. Also Mr. Drew Marley. The brothers all looked like Caucasian men. Then when the church was almost ready to start the service for Walter Marley's funeral, a woman walked in, with another younger woman walking right behind. The both of them walked up to the casket. They stood there for a while, and then one of the women leaned over and kissed Mr. Walter Marley goodbye. The people in the church were in a daze trying to see who these people were.

The service began. Everything was going as planned. It was time for the clerk to read the words of encouragement. "Family, as the day draws near, let us not forget the man that will live in each and every one of your lives. Not just by the seed that will go on and grow forever in an endless time. Let your faith stand strong with love, and may God keep him in his grace and mercy. Amen." Now it was time to read the obituary. "Mr. Walter Marley leaves behind two daughters: Minnie Newton and her husband McKinley Newton, and his daughter Annie Marley of Yazoo Mississippi. Four sons: Selvie Marley, Johnny Marley, Moody, and Cleotha Marley. Three brothers: Drew Marley, Massey Marley, and Will Marley, all of Vicksburg Mississippi. As the obituary was being read, a lot of mumbling could be heard in the church. The service went on for another hour.

Now the pastor has put the last words into the service, and then he said, "Let us pray." After praying, the casket was put in front of the family and they walked behind as the pastor read from Psalm 23. They took Mr. Walter Marley to his final resting place at the local cemetery where he was placed next to his loving wife

Beatrice Draper Marley. After leaving the cemetery, everyone headed back to the church for the dinner.

Pastor White said to everyone, "Please, let us show this family some extra love. They have been through a lot this year losing two family members. So, before we all start to eat, let us pray." Now the prayer was done. Everyone was in line to receive their plate. The food was plentiful, just everything you can think of to eat. The church had pitched in to make this dinner possible. The family and all of the members of the church were served. The family had gotten up and showed the church their gratitude for everyone's love and kindness. Some started to come over to the table where family was.

Now Minnie noticed that the two women that came in the church right before the service started were walking over to her. The one woman was a white woman for sure. The younger woman also looked white or maybe Hispanic. The older one said, "Hi, I'm Annie Marley, Walter's wife." Minnie's brothers were there listening in, and Selvie said in a loud voice, "You were one of his wives. There were many. Yes, we know about you."

Minnie looked over at her brother to say, "Ssshh! Let us listen to what she has to say."

Then the younger woman said, "I'm your sister," as she gave Minnie a hug. Minnie was taken back for a moment, yet she did embrace her sister for the very first time. The brothers all gave her a hug as well. At first, they were not happy with what was said, yet they were thinking that this was not something they could control.

All of the family made their way back to Minnie and McKinley's place. The family was talking and singing well into the late hours of the night. Someone said, "We love you, Mom and Dad. You will never be forgotten."

Now the year was 1938, in November. Selvie was knocking on the door of his sister and brother-in-law's house. He had his wife in the car with him, not sure what to do. His wife, Annie May, was in labor. McKinley answered the door. Selvie explained what was going on. McKinley said, "We need to get Annie to the hospital." The hospital was in Jackson, Mississippi, which was approximately 30 minutes away from Edwards, Mississippi. McKinley had taken over driving for his brother-in-law because it was apparent that Selvie was extremely nervous and was in no condition to do any driving. Now the three of them made their way safely to the hospital. McKinley pulled up to the front door, saying to the both of them, "I will come in as soon as I can find a place to park." Selvie helped his wife inside of the hospital. Now in the waiting room, it took a very long time for the receptionist to check Annie in. Finally the nurse called her name, and she was escorted back to her room. McKinley and Selvie stayed in the waiting room.

Now hours had gone by as the both of them paced back and forth. Every hour Selvie would go up to the reception desk to ask the nurse about the condition of his wife, and she would reply that she was still in labor. After eight hours of this, a nurse came through the door calling his name, "Selvie Marley?"

At this particular time, Selvie was asleep in a chair. McKinley walked over to him and gave him a nudge. "Selvie, they are calling you."

Selvie stood straight up, saying, "Yes, my name is Selvie Marley!"

The nurse said, "Please come with me. You may see your wife now." Selvie asked the nurse, "Is she okay?"

Answering him, "Oh yes! Your wife is fine. Your wife has given birth to a beautiful baby girl."

Selvie followed the nurse to the room where his wife was resting and holding their baby, and he laid his eyes on his daughter for the very first time. He walked over and gave both his wife and then his daughter a kiss. He looked at his wife and said, "Can I hold her?" Annie handed their daughter over to her dad. Selvie was very overwhelmed with emotion. So proud, saying, "Look at her, ten fingers and ten toes, so healthy." He instantly fell in love with his daughter.

The nurse smiled at Selvie and asked, "Do you have a name for her?"

Selvie answered, "We do. Her name is Elise Manley." Selvie held his daughter until the nurses came to take baby Elise back to the nursery. Selvie Manley was so happy about the birth of his child and couldn't wait to share the news with his sister and brothers. McKinley was still in the waiting room. He didn't have a way back home because he had ridden over with his brother-in-law to make sure he was safe. Now that baby and mom were resting, Selvie could give McKinley a ride home and also share the joy of his new baby with his sister, Minnie.

On the way home, the two men had a good conversation, talking about a little of everything. Then the conversation shifted to Selvie's relationship with Stella. Selvie said, "I know that I'm married to Annie, but I just can't leave Stella alone. I don't know what it is. Stella keeps me safe, she holds me accountable for my actions. I just don't know how she will take this."

McKinley said, "Man, you are married to Annie. What do you mean?" Selvie got quiet and changed the subject. McKinley said, "You mean to tell me that Stella thinks it's just you and her?"

Selvie answered, "Well, yes, that's exactly what I'm saying. Man, Stella will kill me." McKinley just smiled at Selvie as the both of them arrived at McKinley's house and walked inside to share the good news of Selvie's first-born child. Selvie called out to his sister, "Minnie, where are you?"

Minnie answered, "I'm in the kitchen cooking."

Selvie had so much joy in his heart about his baby. "I'm a daddy now! I have a baby girl." He was talking loudly, with so much enthusiasm that he could hardly catch his breath. "Yes, we named her Elise. She is so beautiful. I can't wait for you to hold her, Minnie." Minnie smiled at her brother. She was happy for him as well.

Then Minnie said, "Oh, before I forget, Stella came by here this morning wondering if I had seen you and whether you were all right. I told her that I would let you know when I saw you to make sure you contact her."

Selvie answered, "Okay, I will do just that." It was still very early in the morning, and Selvie was sitting in the kitchen with his sister and brother-in-law, enjoying breakfast and a good strong cup of coffee. You could smell the aroma of the coffee wafting throughout the house, which must have gotten the attention of young Robert who walked into the kitchen and said good morning.

Robert turned to his his dad, asking him about them working. "Dad, you know that we have missed two days of work this week."

McKinley did not like the fact that his son was questioning him about what he was doing. Talking to his son in a very loud voice, he answered, "You don't come in here asking me anything! Besides that, I am the man in this house, so if you don't like the way things are being run here, you know where the door is."

Robert talked back and told his dad that he didn't have to use that tone with him, also saying to his dad, "How are you going to tell me anything? I don't need you." And he walked out of the house, slamming the door behind him.

McKinley was left speechless. Then he turned to Minnie and said, "You had better get him before I tan his hide!"

Minnie looked at McKinley and said, "Give him some time. He is still grieving the death of my parents." McKinley just walked away mumbling.

Selvie said to Minnie, "Let me talk to Robert." Robert was outside sitting in his uncle's truck. Selvie walked over to Robert and said to him, "Now, what are you going to do?"

Robert said, "Well, I'm going to go get me a job."

Selvie said, "A job? You may be as tall as I am, but you are still a child."

Robert answered, "No, I am a man. I will show you! I have already looked into this. I asked Mr. Roy Brintal if I could work in town pumping gas."

Selvie said, "You know that you are only nine years old?"

"Yes, I know. I have to take care of myself because my dad doesn't care for me. I don't even believe that he loves me. So, if you would, could you please give me a ride into town? I'm going to the gas station."

Selvie said, "Yes, I will."

Robert went into the house and gathered up his things. On his way out the door, he looked into the kitchen where his mother was standing. Robert looked his mom in the eyes and then gave her a hug as if he didn't want to go. He said, "Bye, Mom!"

Minnie said to her son, "Bye, son," hoping that he would change his mind. But Robert was so determined in his decision. He walked out the door and got in the truck with his uncle.

As they made their way down the road, Selvie said, "So, nephew, you know it's not too late to change your mind."

"I know I can. I just can't stay here. They don't have any place for me. I have to make it on my own."

"I will make sure to check on you and make sure that you are eating."

Robert looked over at his uncle and smiled. Finally, they arrived at the gas station, and Selvie and his nephew got out of the truck. They walked inside the store. Robert walked over to Mr. Roy Brintal and asked him about the job he had promised him.

Mr. Roy Brintal said to him, "When can you start, boy?"

Robert had to take a deep breath before answering. "Well, I can start today."

"I can only pay you 20 dollars a week. Okay, boy, I know your family, so I know that they are somewhat honest people. I can trust that you won't steal from me."

"Oh, no, I won't."

"Boy, one more thing you need to know."

"Yes, what is it?"

"You need to answer me with 'sir.' I hope I make myself clear."

"Oh, oh, yes, sir, it won't happen again."

"Well, I hope that it won't be a problem or I'm going to have to let you go."

"Okay, yes, sir."

"There is a seat in front of the store. You are to sit there until a customer pulls up. Then you will walk up to their window and ask them, 'May I help you, sir or ma'am?' Then pump the gas that they ask for, then take the money into the store and give it to me or whoever is working inside the store."

"Okay, yes, sir."

"Okay, you can start now."

"Yes, sir."

Robert's uncle Selvie was standing in the door waiting to see if he would change his mind. Then the two of them walked outside and Robert took a seat. His uncle said, "Where are you going to stay?"

"Well, I have a room here."

His uncle said, "Oh, really?"

Robert answered, "Yes, I do."

"Well, I have to go check on my wife," said Selvie. "I will check on you tomorrow.

Robert said, "I will see you then." His uncle gave him 5 dollars before he pulled off.

Robert worked all day at the gas station. It was getting late, and Robert was getting thirsty. In the front of the store was a barrel of water. A cup hung from the side of the barrel. Robert had been giving the customers a drink from this cup all day. Mr. Brintal had been watching Robert from afar. Robert, being so thirsty, had taken the cup and dipped it into the water and taken a drink.

Mr. Roy Brintal waited until Robert was finished drinking, and then he walked over to him and said in a very loud voice, "What the hell are you doing?"

Robert looked at Mr. Roy Brintal and said, "I was getting myself a drink. I have been working all day."

"Well, I want you to know that you will have to pour all of that water out of the barrel and scrub it down with soap and disinfectant because we can't have a nigger drinking our of the same barrel as the whites."

Robert was so very hurt, but he kept his emotions to himself and said, "Yes, sir, it won't happen again."

"When you need a drink, you go on the side where you get water for your nigger customers."

"Okay, yes, sir." Now Robert had done what was asked of him to do, and it was time for him to go home. Where was home? Robert had only 5 dollars in his pocket. He was really hungry. There was a restaurant inside the gas station. Robert had paid very close attention to the Black people using the back door. There was a counter where they would sit down and order their food. Robert walked through the back door and sat down at the counter. The cook asked him what he would like and handed him a menu to read. Robert looked it up and down, then he answered the cook, "Well, can I have pancakes and then a glass of milk, please?"

"Yes," the cook answered.

The cook handed Robert his meal, and he said, "Thank you."

The cook was a Black man. He asked Robert, "What are you doing here? Shouldn't you be home with your parents? You're McKinley's son, right?"

Robert nodded yes. He sat there eating his meal really slowly. Robert finished eating and then said, "Okay, I will see you tomorrow." As he walked out the door, Robert realized that he had nowhere to go. He needed to be back bright and early the next day, so he decided to sleep behind the garage. The night was cold and very dark, and it was hard to fall asleep. He could hear dogs barking and owls hooting. He could hear crickets chirping. Looking out into the night with nothing but the moon for light, he could barely see his hand in front of his fact.

Robert lay there for awhile, and then he heard footsteps coming his way! He began to shake with fear. Then a very loud voice called out, "Who is back there? I have myself a gun. Don't make me have to shoot you. Come out NOW!"

Robert stood up, holding his hands over his head. "Please don't shoot!"

Robert saw that it was the cook. He said, "What on earth are you doing back here?"

Robert said, "I have nowhere to go."

The cook said, "Come with me. I live upstairs. You can sleep in my room tonight. There is a very small room that Mr. Roy Brintal has for rent. It will cost you 10 dollars a week. How does that sound? Now, you know that you can't sleep out here. You could get bitten by a snake or a wolf."

Robert said, "Thank you." Then he asked the cook, "What is your name?"   "My name is Willie-James. You can call me Will." Now Will took Robert upstairs to his room and gave him a pillow and a blanket. He only had the floor to offer him, yet it was better than sleeping outside. Robert got himself comfortable, and Will said, "Get yourself some sleep. I'm going outside to the porch to have myself a drink and a smoke. I will be back real soon." Before Will had even left, Robert had fallen asleep after working a very long and hard day.

Bright and early the next morning, Robert was up and made his way downstairs. He was in his position and ready to pump gas. Mr. Brintal walked past Robert, and Robert said, "Good morning, sir." Mr. Brintal was on his way to the kitchen to get his breakfast that was already cooked for him. Mr. Brintal was very predicable. He was like a clock. You know where he was almost all the time.

Robert was going in and out of the store, doing his job, when he ran into Mr. Will. Mr. Will said to Robert, "Hold on, young buck. What have you eaten today?"

Robert looked up at Mr. Will and answered, "Well, nothing."

"You know it is very important to take care of yourself. Now, you can't run around here and not eat. I will make you something. Tell me what you would like." Mr. Will handed Robert the menu. Robert scanned it quickly and then passed it back to Mr. Will. In his next breath, he said, "I would like pancakes."

Mr. Will said to him, "Son, you can't read, can you?"

Robert put his head down and answered him. "No, no, I can't. I always order pancakes because I know that everyone had them on their menu. So that way nobody has any idea that I can't read."

"Well, if it were up to me, you would be in school instead of here working." Over the next few months, Mr. Will kept a very close eye on Robert, helping him in any way he could. The both of them worked very hard each and every day. After they had closed up for the night, Mr. Will would take out his harmonica and play the blues. The blues gave many Black people comfort in their everyday lives. Mr. Will also had a five-string guitar. Robert would pick it up and he would feel the music. He taught himself how to play. The both of them would play for hours. They were both very good at it too. So, when Robert wasn't working, he was into his music.

Meanwhile, six months had gone by. One day, McKinley came into town to shop and get gas. He saw his son Robert. McKinley got out of his truck. Robert walked over to where his dad was standing and said, "Good morning, can I pump you some gas?" in the same way he would address the other customers.

McKinley said, "I would like a dollar of gas, and that will last me a long time." At the time, gas was 10 cents a gallon. McKinley didn't say anything else to his son. After Robert finished pumping his gas, McKinley got back into his truck. Robert watched him drive down the until he couldn't see him anymore and the dust of the road had made him disappear. McKinley made it home after a long day's work in the fields. He walked into the house and went over to his wife, Minnie, and gave her a hug and a big kiss. Most of the time, Minnie was in the kitchen cooking. The two older children would help their mother prepare dinner and help out with the younger children who were all over the place playing and laughing. McKinley said to his wife, "I saw our son today. He was working at Roy Brintal's gas station. He was there pumping gas!"

Minnie asked, "How is he doing? When are you going to ask him to come home?"

"Well, Minnie, he has gotten too big for his britches. I can't discipline him like I want to. My son says that he is a man now. I have to respect that."

Minnie said, "He is your son. I don't like the fact that you don't spend any time with your son."

"I'm sorry, Minnie. I will see if he would like to go church with us on Sunday."

"That would be nice." Minnie was done cooking and setting the table for dinner. It was time to eat, and the family sat down all together. Minnie was very quiet. She also looked a little under the weather. She was trying to hold it all together.

Her husband asked, "Minnie, are you okay?"

She answered, "Yes, I'm fine." Now everyone was done with dinner. Minnie and her older two girls started to clear the table. Minnie picked up some dished, stood up, and turned away from the table. She took a few steps, lost her balance, and dropped the dishes on the floor, breaking them all.

McKinley jumped out of his seat and rushed over to his wife. He had his arm around his wife, looking her in her eyes. He said, "Tell me what is wrong. Minnie, whatever it is, we will get through it."

Minnie looked in her husband's eyes, saying, "I know that we have eight children. Well, we are going to have one more." McKinley was in shock. Minnie said to McKinley, "Did you hear me?"

He paused for a moment, then he said, "This is wonderful." He helped Minnie to bed so she could rest. The children, with the help of their dad, finished cleaning up the kitchen and helped everyone settle down for the night.

The year was 1939. Franklin D. Roosevelt was president. He was a Democrat who would serve four terms as president. As for Black people's lives, in Mississippi, the times were very difficult. Agriculture had collapsed, and work was scarce. The state of Mississippi was seriously divided when it came to the outlook on race. McKinley still worked for Mr. Roy Brintal. He would work odd jobs, and he also worked as a sharecropper. He knew that he had to provide for his family.

On September 1, 1939, Hitler invaded Poland, and then, two days later, France and Britain declared war on Germany. This was the beginning of World War II. McKinley knew that his wife would be giving birth to their ninth child very soon. Minnie was suffering with difficulties of her diabetes, and McKinley didn't want to take any chances with his wife's health. McKinley remembered the stories about his biological mother giving birth and losing her life.

A month had gone by. McKinley stayed close by Minnie's side, keeping a close eye on her, waiting for the right time to go to the hospital, which was in the city of Jackson, Mississippi. On November 25, 1939, Minnie and McKinley welcomed the newest member of their family, a baby girl named Dorothy Mae Newton.

McKinley would just hold this baby, always letting everyone know how precious she was.

After spending a week in the hospital, it was time for Minnie and her baby to go home. One never knew what God had for our future. After they pulled up to the house, McKinley walked out to the road to check the mailbox. He looked through the mail. One letter stood out. It was from the government. On the front of the envelope was McKinley's full name and the words "Uncle Sam Wants You." McKinley opened it up and started to read. It said that he needed to report to his local recruiting office. McKinley had been drafted! He stood there for a moment. He took his hat off and scratched his head. He had mixed emotions. On the one hand, he was excited, but on the other hand, he was fearful. He thought about all he could do for his family. He also thought about the fact that Black men in the military were subject to the Jim Crow laws. The letter said that McKinley should show up for further information on Thursday, December 7, 1939.

McKinley went into the house to share the news with his wife. Minnie showed her husband support by listening to him, and they talked about the pros and cons of him going to war. Meanwhile, Selvie came by to see the new baby. He had his daughter, Elise, with him, who had just started to walk. Selvie had come by for only a few minutes to inform his sister about Uncle Miles's children who would be visiting soon from Chicago. Selvie also let Minnie know that he went to check on their son Robert each and every day. "Oh, and before I forget, me and my baby, Stella, will be going to Las Vegas, Nevada," Selvie said. "Yes, Stella has a job as a cook out there, making some big money." He walked out the door, talking loudly, "Well, Sis and McKinley, congratulations on your new baby!" McKinley sat on the porch of his home watching as Selvie drove off into the sunset.

A few days later, it was December 7, 1940, the day that McKinley was to report to the recruiting office at 7:00 AM. McKinley was up by 5:00 AM. Yes, like always, Minnie was up preparing his breakfast. When McKinley walked out the door, everyone else was still asleep. The closest recruiting office was in Jackson, Mississippi. When McKinley finally arrived at the office, he stood outside looking at the door. He took a deep breath first and then walked into a large gymnasium. On the other side of this gym were desks with clerks sitting at them. McKinley walked up to a clerk, holding his papers in his hand. "Hi, my name is McKinley Newton. I want to make sure that I'm in the right place. Could you please check for me?"

The man answered, "Yes, you are in the right place." He handed McKinley a t-shirt and some shorts. "There's a locker room down the hallway. You need to put your things in the locker that was assigned to you. Then come back out to the gym and stand on one of the X's on the floor." By the time McKinley had gotten back to the gym, almost all of the X's on the floor had been taken.

McKinley stood on one of the X's, patiently waiting for his instructions. Eventually, a man walked in front of the group. He said, "Good morning. My name is Sergeant Fisher. I will be checking to see if you have any physical disabilities, making sure all of you are able to bend over and touch your toes. When we are done with this, we will go to the next stage. Then, before you leave, I will call you over and let you know your next move. At that point, you will know your assignment. Now, if you pass all of the tests put before you, most likely you will be sent to boot camp. This is where you will do some intense training. This purpose of the training is to prepare you for the war."

McKinley passed every task that was given to him. Now it was time to have a one-on-one conversation, so Sergeant Fisher called out in a very loud voice, "McKinley Newton!" Sergeant Fisher had McKinley's application in his hand. McKinley sat down to talk, and Sergeant Fisher said, "I see that you finished high school. You also have some college under your belt."

McKinley answered, "Yes, sir."

Sergeant Fisher paused for a moment and said, "I see here that you have nine children."

McKinley said, "Yes, sir," very proudly.

Sergeant Fisher walked away for about two minutes and then returned. His next words were, "I'm sorry, but there is no way I can allow you to join the military." McKinley looked at the sergeant with a puzzled look on his face. He knew that he had passed the tests and tasks set before him. The sergeant said, "Well, as of today, you are dismissed."

McKinley said, "May I ask why, sir?"

"You have too many children. I can't allow you to join because the government is not going to pay your wife that kind of money as a negro. We will not pay that kind of money to people of your kind. I have dismissed your application. You will no longer have to report." So McKinley gathered up his things and made his way back to his truck. He sat there shaking his head, thinking, trying to make sense of what had happened. On the one hand, he wanted to go and fight for his country and also try to provide a living for his family. On the other hand, he felt relieved. God has something else for me, he thought.

Approximately 463,000 Black men served in World War II. Men who took pride in their country! Yet their country often treated them like second-class citizens. The press affectionately called the Black soldiers "tan soldiers." Imagine having to fight racism at home in the United States of America and then fighting the enemy abroad! McKinley went back to work as always, making a living for his family. They prayed for things to get better, while they took care of eight of their nine children.

They continued to attend church, and bright and early one Sunday morning, everyone was up and ready for church. They all piled in the truck and drove to church. When McKinley, his wife and children walked into the church, he heard someone call out his name: "McKinley! McKinley!" He turned to see who it was, and lo and behold it was his brother, Jonathan Brooks, Jr. They embraced each other with the biggest hug.

McKinley said, "Man, it's good to see you."

Jonathan said, "It's good to see you as well. I'm so glad that I was able to find you. Your father, Henry Nixon, was inquiring as to your whereabouts. He wants you to contact him. He wants to give you some land. I won't keep you--here is an address and the information."

McKinley said to his brother, "Come on and join me in church and come over for dinner this evening, please. I want you to meet my family."

Jonathan replied, "I'm so sorry, but I can't make it today. I promise that I will make it up to you." The both of them hugged and said "See you soon" as they parted ways.

Later on that day, after dinner was all over with, McKinley shared with his wife the information that his brother had given him earlier that day. Minnie asked, "Well, are you going to call him?"

McKinley answered, "Let me think about it. You know that this is long-distance and it will cost us money." Minnie knew how much this meant to her husband. She was thinking that he didn't want to call out of fear of being rejected. Not trying to make him upset, she said, "If it makes you feel better, we can pray

about it. Then God will lead you to what you need to do next."
Minnie took her husband's hand and they began to pray. Their
prayer was long and passionate. Their prayer was very tearful.
Now, they ended their prayer, "in Jesus' name, Amen."

McKinley sat still for a few minutes, and then he decided to
make the call of his life. As he dialed the number, he took a deep
breath. The phone was ringing! After about the fifth ring, a
woman on the other end of the line said, "Hello."

McKinley's voice, a little shaky, said, "Hello, my name is
McKinley. May I please speak to Henry Nixon? I was told to give
him a call."

"Oh, hi, sugar, I'm your auntie, your daddy's sister. You
can call me Mary!"

"Uh, okay, Miz Mary."

"No, sweetie, you can call me your auntie Mary."

McKinley said, "Okay, Auntie Mary."

She said, "Now, that's better. The reason that your dad
wanted you to call him was he wants you to come to Memphis,
Tennessee. You have other brothers and they will all be here. I
believe he wants to divide some land that he has before he moves
up north. I need to know whether you can make it here. McKinley
said that he would love to come but that he couldn't afford the trip
with a family as big as his was. He also told her that because he
was the only one working, there was no way he would be able to
afford it. Auntie Mary said to McKinley, "Say no more. I will
send you a train ticket. You know that I do not know what you
look like, so please call me back and tell me the date you will
arrive. When you get off the train, I need you to put a red
handkerchief in your front pocket. I will make sure someone will
be there to pick you up. They will bring you to my house."

McKinley said, "Thank you, Auntie Mary! I will be
waiting. I will talk to you real soon." As the both of them hung up

the phone, McKinley was so excited, calling out to his wife, Minnie, grabbing her by the hands. He was jumping for joy, full of love and happiness in his heart, repeating to himself, "I'm going to Memphis, Tennessee!" McKinley was also telling Minnie that he wouldn't be gone too long, and reassuring her that going to Memphis was for the good of the family. His heart was so full of joy! This was something that McKinley had waited on for so long. He would finally get the chance to meet his father, Mr. Henry Nixon. The night was getting away from everyone. Now, lying in bed listening to the quiet sound of the night, he held his wife in his arms as they fell fast asleep.

    A week had gone by. This bright sunny Saturday morning, McKinley was up early. Up doing chores and talking and playing with his children. His son, Junior, whom he had named after himself, had asked his dad if they could have chicken for dinner that night. Junior was only 10 years old. His dad answered, "Go ask your mother."

    He replied, "Okay, Dad!" So Junior made his way from the yard into the house. "Hey, Mom, can we please have chicken tonight for dinner?"

    "No, not tonight. The taste would be very different, because you have to feed chickens special grain before you kill them to eat. Maybe next week, okay?" answered his mother.

    Junior went outside in the yard where his other siblings were, mumbling under his breath, "They said I can't have any chicken." Saying to himself and his sister Ann, "I betcha I will have me some chicken!"

    In the meantime, his dad was checking the mailbox, and he pulled out four letters. One was from Auntie Mary! McKinley was so excited that he had to go back into the house where Minnie was. He wanted to share the news with her. "Look, Minnie! It's the letter I was telling you about. I have been waiting on this for a while." McKinley opened up the letter. It was a train ticket to Memphis. The ticket was for a Saturday in two weeks' time. "Yes, this will give me time to get everything in order. I need to ask for a few days off of work." McKinley sat talking with Minnie. "Our daughter Beatrice will help you do what needs to be done." Minnie looked at McKinley and smiled at him. Then they heard a loud commotion in the yard.

The chickens would walk around the yard of their own free will, minding their own business. Junior had tied a piece of corn to a string. Then he had pulled this string through a hole in the porch. Then he had placed himself under the porch, holding the string in his hand. He was patiently waiting for the moment when one of the chickens would nibble on his bait. Oh, wait, one has fallen for his trap! Now, with the corn in the chicken's mouth and also on the string, Junior pulled on the string real hard, which broke the chicken's neck. Junior came out from under the porch, making sure that he had gotten rid of his evidence. The chicken was lying on the porch, dead. McKinley and Minnie came outside and saw the dead chicken on the porch. Minnie said, "We can't afford to waste any food." She asked McKinley, "Can you please go and clean this chicken up for dinner tonight?"

Junior was standing in the yard, looking as if he didn't know what was going on. His sister was standing by his side. Junior gave her a nudge and said to her, "I told you we were going to have some chicken for dinner."

Two weeks had gone by. McKinley was up early and all ready for his trip to Memphis. Minnie was also up, preparing breakfast for her husband. She said to him, "I prepared you a lunch so you can save money on your trip. You may have to get a room to stay in or something."

McKinley was waiting for his friend Rudy to take him to the train station. There was a knock at the door. It was Rudy. He said, "I'm here to take you to the train station."

McKinley said to Rudy, "I will be out in a few minutes." McKinley grabbed his bag and he put his arms around his wife, hugging her and giving her a real big kiss. "Minnie, this will be a big change in our lives."

Minnie said, "Be careful."

McKinley walked out the door and he and Rudy drove to the train station where Rudy dropped him off. As he approached the platform, McKinley got his ticket out of his pocket. The train conductor was calling, "All aboard for Memphis, Tennessee!" McKinley handed the conductor his ticket, and the conductor pointed McKinley toward the section assigned for people of color. The white people sat up front and were taken care of very nicely.

The ride to Memphis would be a 10-hour ride, with the train stopping at lots of stations along the way. The train was all steamed up and ready to go. Everyone was in their seats. McKinley was thinking out loud, "I'm going to see my birth dad! Wow, I'm excited." He looked around at his fellow passengers. There was a young lady with three children who were keeping their mom busy, crying and asking a lot of questions. One of the children said, "Mom, I'm hungry." They had nothing to eat. The young mother said, "We will be at grandma's house real soon." McKinley couldn't help overhearing the children crying out that they were hungry. McKinley said hello to the young lady and asked her, "When was the last time you and your children ate?" He added, "I didn't get your name?"

The young lady replied, "My name is Mary Anne."

"I'm sorry, I just couldn't ignore the fact that you and your children are hungry. Please let me help. My beautiful wife made me a huge lunch. I know that God would want me to do the right thing. I believe that God puts people in certain places at certain times. It's like he knows what a person needs. So, here, feed your children. I'm okay, I had a very big breakfast. Here's two dollars as well. I know it's not much, yet I know it will get you a meal for the kids."

Mary Ann said, "Thank you, thank you so much." She had tears in her eyes. McKinley could see that she was so grateful. The children were also pleased. They had stopped bickering. McKinley was very happy to help. He felt compelled to help. It broke his heart to see this situation. He said the young lady reminded him of one of his daughters.

The ride was long, and there were others on this train to Memphis. A man who was sitting in the back looked over to McKinley and said, "Man, that was a very nice thing you did, helping this young family out. It's funny, you said your name is McKinley? Well, that's my name, too. My name is McKinley Morgafield. They call me Muddy Waters. I'm from Mississippi. I'm on my way to Memphis to see what's going on with the blues. I want to go to this street, I believe it's called Beal Street. I'm supposed to meet a man named Alan there, we'll see! Hey, tell me something. Can you sing?"

McKinley Newton said, "Yes, I think so." So that's when Muddy started to play a song that a lot of people knew, "Mary, don't you weep, tell Martha don't you moan. Yes, Jesus said, Mary don't you weep, tell Martha not to moan. Pharaoh's army had gotten drowned in the Red Sea." From this point on, the music kept them entertained the rest of the way to Memphis. McKinley would never forget that day. Everyone in that section of the box car of the train had fallen asleep. By the time morning came, the conductor was making the announcement that the train would be pulling into Memphis shortly. Now McKinley was really excited. He gathered up his things so he could get ready to exit the train. The train arrived at the station around 8:00 AM. McKinley reached into his back pocket to get his red handkerchief. He put it in his front pocket so proudly. He got off the train and was standing on the platform, looking around for someone to make eye contact with. After a while, everyone else who had gotten off the train had made their way to their destination. McKinley kept looking at the clock at the station. It was now 10:00 AM. No one had come for him. Finally, it was well past 4:00 PM and most of the day had gone by. McKinley had a phone number and address in his suitcase. With only 20 dollars to his name, he got into one of the taxi cabs. He asked the nice man if he would take him to the address on the paper. The taxi driver took him to the place on Madison Street. After having a very nice conversation with the taxi driver, the driver said, "We are here. Good luck, man," as he pulled away.

McKinley stood in front of a huge house. He was trying not to be scared, yet he was. He took a moment and said a prayer. Then he took a deep breath and proceeded to make his way to the front door. He knocked. The door opened up right away. A woman stood there. She said, "Oh, my goodness! You must be Henry Nixon's son, you look just like him." She threw her arms around him. "Baby, I'm your Auntie Mary. I'm so sorry, someone was supposed to have picked you up. I thought you were coming tomorrow. Baby, come on in. Are you hungry? Would you like something to drink? You drink whiskey?

McKinley said, "Yes, I would love something to eat. I don't drink whiskey or moonshine. I would like some water or a soda."

"Sure, baby." Now I have some good news and some bad news. The good news is that you can stay here and eat anything you want. The bad news is that your dad, Henry Nixon, and your brothers won't be able to make it here to see you. Not at this time. He has some very pressing business in Chicago. He wanted me to apologize to you. He also wants to make up for it as well.

McKinley had a very disappointed look on his face as he answered his auntie, "Yes, ma'am." Auntie Mary's house that McKinley stayed at seemed to him to be a party house, a place where everyone would come and go as they pleased. The music would be playing from sunup to sundown. McKinley wanted to see if he could develop a relationship with his auntie Mary. He asked her to tell him about his dad.

Mary answered, "What is it you would like to know?"

"What his life was like up until now, his likes and dislikes. The places he may have gone. Tell me about how many children he has. About his children, all of them. I always wanted brothers and sisters. When I was growing up, I had no one to play with. I had no one to talk to, no one to share my secrets with. I had two loving parents, but it wasn't enough. I only found out later in life that I have siblings."

"Well, son, your father was a married man. I really didn't know about you until your dad moved from the South and wanted to live in a very big city, so he moved to Chicago. Henry is my little brother. I have always tried to look out for him. I now have the pleasure of getting better acquainted with you. I don't want this to be the only time that I see you. I want you to call me at least once a week. I want to know about my great-nieces and nephews. How many children do you have?"

"I have nine children, seven girls and two boys."

"That is wonderful. I'm sure that your father will be so happy to know this. Henry doesn't know that he is a grandpa. I can't wait to tell him."

"Well, Auntie Mary, I was so elated to meet the man whom they say is my father. Well, now that I won't have the chance to meet him, it is just a very devastating feeling for me. So now what, Auntie Mary? What's going to happen?"

"Well, sweetie, y'all will meet him, trust me. Oh, I have something for you. Your dad left this envelope with your name on it."

McKinley took the envelope and looked at it for a few moments. Then he slowly opened it up. Inside were five one-hundred-dollar bills. McKinley said, "WOW, are you sure this is for me?"

Auntie Mary said, "Yes, I really am sure. I don't know if you know a lot about your father, or dad, but trust me, he can afford to give this to you. I'm sure it will help you with a few things."

"Yes, Auntie, it will help our family. The children need new shoes. Wow, I can buy my wife a new dress for church. I can't wait to get back home and show them."

"When are you leaving, McKinley?"

"I'm going to leave in the morning. We will invite you to come see us in Mississippi sometime."

"I would love to come. I can't wait to see your lovely wife and my great-nieces and nephews."

"Thank you, Auntie Mary, for letting me stay here. I really appreciate your hospitality." McKinley said his good-nights to everyone who was sitting in the living room, and before he retired to the room that was for him, he thanked Aunt Mary again. "Oh, I won't wake you up. I will catch the train back to Jackson, Mississippi in the morning."

"How will you get to the train station?"

"Well, Auntie, I can get a taxi."

"McKinley, I will get up and take you. Let me do that. I really feel bad enough that Henry Nixon couldn't be here. I also feel bad that no one was at the train station to pick you up. So please let me help."

"Okay, Auntie. I'm leaving here at 5:00 AM. The train will leave the station at 6:30 AM. Are you sure you want to do this?"

"Yes! Baby, I will be up before you. I will see you bright and early in the morning."

McKinley said, "Okay, Auntie. I'm going to sleep now. See you in the morning."

It was now 5:00 AM and McKinley was gathering up his things, washing his face in the bathroom. Then he went downstairs to find his Auntie Mary fast asleep on the sofa. McKinley took a moment to write a brief letter thanking her for everything. He ended his letter with, "I love you, and hope to see you soon." McKinley folded up the letter and placed it on his auntie's lap. He gave her a kiss on her forehead. There was a phone in the kitchen, and he called for a taxi. Then he went outside on the porch to wait for the arrival of his ride. It wasn't long before the taxi pulled up. Now off he went to the train station. McKinley made it to the station just in the nick of time. The train conductor was calling out for the last call. "All aboard! All aboard for Jackson, Mississippi!"

McKinley already had his ticket in his hand as he ran for the train, yelling "Wait! Wait! I'm going to Jackson, sir." The conductor took his ticket as McKinley walked up the stairs and found his way to his seat. The train left shortly thereafter. McKinley had a long ride ahead of him. Yet he knew that he would be home late that night or very early the next morning. As he was sitting on the train contemplating his trip, he was thinking that it wasn't all a loss. He had the pleasure of meeting his auntie, and he had also been given some money. He knew that 500 dollars would do a lot for his family. So, he spent the train ride trying to occupy his mind by reading a book that he had in his pocket. Then, by looking out at the countryside, and seeing how beautiful the scenery was. Then, falling asleep. He would repeat this over and over again. His trip was well over 10 hours long.

Finally, McKinley made it back to Jackson, Mississippi, and called his friend for a ride home. McKinley arrived home to his wife and children. He was so happy to see them all. He told everyone all that he had experienced on his trip. As he was looking at his wife, he noticed that Minnie had a glow about herself. He was thinking, Is she pregnant again? Then he said to himself, "Naw, we already have nine children." As he was talking to himself, "Get this thought out of my head," Minnie was calling McKinley. He was deep in his thoughts as she repeated his name three times. He finally answered her.

"I made you some dinner. Are you hungry?"

He answered, "Yes, I am. I would like that." Now the both of them were sitting at the table. McKinley said to his wife, "Well, if I didn't know any better, I would think that you are pregnant again."

Minnie didn't say anything. Then she said, real slowly, "Well, yes I am. We are expecting this baby sometime in the new year of 1941."

McKinley took a deep breath, and then he said, "Well, just one more mouth to feed, my happy family." He got up and gave Minnie a real big hug, not really happy about the news. He knew his part in the situation and that Minnie hadn't done it by herself.

McKinley walked outside and sat down on the porch for most of the night just thinking how he could provide a better life for his wife and children. Minnie walked out the door and sat next to her husband. She reached over and held his hand, and the both of them sat with their heads pressed up against each other. Minnie asked, "What's wrong?"

McKinley looked at his wife and said, "I always wanted a big family, I just never imagined that God would bless me with the riches of love by giving me the gift of having such a beautiful family. I am so grateful. I know that it's hard now, yet I can see that our children will spread their lives all over this world. I know that the sky is the limit." Minnie just sat there and agreed with what he said. They sat there next to each other for a long time, looking into the sky at the big, beautiful moon with a sprinkle of stars as the night came upon them.

It was the summer of 1941. Minnie and McKinley were blessed with the birth of their tenth child. The proud parents were so happy. It was a baby girl. Her name was Mary Alice Newton.

But while the family was getting bigger, the house was getting smaller. One morning, with the commotion of the birth of the new baby, Beatrice, one of the older girls, was on her way outside to get some eggs for breakfast. Beatrice, by the way, was only 12 years old and soon to be 13 years old in the fall. As she walked out the door and onto the porch, she saw her little sister Elizabeth all curled up in a blanket, lying next to their dog. Beatrice said to Elizabeth, "Is that you?"

Elizabeth answered her sister, with tears streaming down her face. "I had nowhere to go! There was no more room for me in Momma's room. Momma has a new baby!"

Beatrice looked at Elizabeth and told her, "You will always have a place to sleep. You can come sleep with me in my bed." Even though there were only two bedrooms in the house, the room the children slept in was a very large room. Yet there were four people to a bed. The younger children slept in the room with their mom and dad. Beatrice told Elizabeth never to worry again, and she let her know that she would always take care of her, which she did.

Beatrice was the second oldest child, so she was given a lot of responsibility. It wasn't long before she had taken on the duty of cleaning the house and cooking breakfast and dinner as well. It wasn't enough that she was called upon to be a substitute teacher when a teacher was absent. Beatrice was also a Sunday School teacher. She also make sure that everyone's clothes were clean, washing them in a tub by hand, and then hanging them on the line to air dry.

Some people couldn't understand why Beatrice had to do so much work. They said that her mother would just lie in bed. Some thought Minnie was just downright lazy. The fact of the matter was that Minnie was suffering from an illness called diabetes. In the South, they called this disease "sugar." The year 1922 was the first time that there was a treatment administered for diabetes. Insulin was discovered by Sir Frederick G. Banting and Charles H. Best, also J.R. MacLead at the University of Toronto in 1921 and it was purified later on in the year of 2010 by James B. Collip. Now before there was insulin, the only thing that could be done for diabetes was to put people on a very strict diet and keep track of their carbohydrate intake. The life expectancy of a person with diabetes was very short. It's also something most likely inherited from one's parents or ancestors.

One day, McKinley received a letter in the mail letting him know that his family would be coming from Chicago, Illinois. It was Uncle Miles and his family, who wanted to see what it was like living in a big city. They were letting McKinley and Minnie know that they would be coming to visit them in Mississippi within the next six months. In the meantime, everyday life went on with the family getting so big. The older children were very busy.

Minnie's step-sister would come over to visit the children as well. They called her Auntie Marley. She loved her sister, yet when she came over to visit, she would always be very critical of her sister's house and children being unclean. Auntie Marley had taken a shine to Minnie and McKinley's oldest daughter, Christine. Christine was influenced by Auntie Marley at a very early age. She was now 14 years old, and she was beautiful. Auntie Marley also made Christine feel a sense of privilege. Auntie Marley was into education, being a principal of one of the schools in Mississippi, and she was always telling Christine that she was going to be a nurse one day. "So keep your head in the books. I will make sure that you go to college. Yes, you will get your license in nursing." Auntie Marley said she would be sure to make that happen. Auntie Marley had connections that others in the family did not have access to.

One Sunday, like every other Sunday, McKinley piled his children and wife into the truck. They attended church faithfully each and every Sunday. The sky was so blue, and the heat was on in the south of Mississippi that day. The family walked into church together. One of the church members said to McKinley, "Wow, your children are all growing up so fast. It was just yesterday that the little ones could barely walk. Now, look at them so big. I know that you are so pleased."

McKinley replied, "Yes, I'm very proud," as he made his way up to give devotions. He had on his Sunday-best shoes, his only pair of dress shoes. You could hear the heels of his shoes click, click, click on the hardwood floor. Christine was sitting close to her mother as her father was reading from the Bible. The congregation all had their heads bowed. Christine lifted her head, and noticed that sitting on the other side of the church was a young man who had his eyes fixed on her. He couldn't stop looking at her; he was not even paying attention to what was going on in the service. Christine just gave him a very big smile. The choir started to sing the song "There's a leak in this old building and my soul has got to move."

After about an hour of the service Pastor White dismissed the church. As everyone made their way to the parking lot, the young man who had had his eyes glued to Christine walked over to her dad's truck. He said, "Hi. Hi, my name is Earl, Earl Lindsey. Your name is Christine, right?" Christine blushed and put her head down. He continued, "Say, can we go out for a soda today?"

Christine looked up and said, "I have to ask my parents."

Earl said, "Okay, I will wait right here while you find out if you can go." Christine walked over to her mom and asked whether it would be okay for her to go out with some of the other kids from church to get a soda. Fearing their disapproval, she didn't tell her mom or dad that she was actually going out with the young man from church.

Her mother said, "Well, don't stay out too long with your friends. You should be home for dinner, right?"

Christine answered, "Yes, Mom, I will be home for dinner," and she walked over to where Earl was standing on the other side of the church by his truck. It was around 2:00 PM. Earl walked around the truck and got in on the driver's side. The two of them drove to the gas station that was close by. At this time, Christine's brother Robert was still working very hard at the gas station. Yes, he also still lived over the store as well. Earl pulled up to the side of the gas station where colored people were served. He got out of his truck and went inside the store.

Robert couldn't help seeing his sister in the truck with this young man. He walked over to the truck and knocked on the window. Christine saw that it was her brother. Robert said, "I know that your dad doesn't know you are out with this man."

Christine replied, "Uh-huh, yes he does."

Robert said, "I really don't believe that."

Christine said to Robert, "This is none of your business." Robert walked away and went back to pumping gas.

While Robert had been so distracted by his sister, a truck had pulled up. The driver asked, "Can you fill it up for me? I believe it will last me for about a week." Robert turned around because the voice sounded oh so familiar--it was his uncle Marley who jumped out of his truck and gave his nephew a great big hug. The both of them hadn't seen each other for at least two years. Selvie Marley was back from Las Vegas, Nevada. Robert was surprised to see him since Selvie had walked away and vowed he wouldn't look back. He said, "The big-city life just isn't for me and Stella. That is why we are back in Mississippi. I also needed to check on you, and I missed my baby girl as well. I hear that Elise stays over to your parents' house a lot."

Robert asked, "How long have you been back in town?"

"Well, I just got in town today. I'm headed over to your parents' house now." Robert couldn't get over the fact that Selvie was back and also that his sister was out with a young man. He wanted their dad to know about this too.

Later on that evening, Minnie was sitting on her porch when she heard the gravel making a cracking sound and the dust popping up from truck tires rolling down the road. This truck slowly approached the pavement in front of their home and stopped. Minnie was sitting in her rocking chair, and she stopped rocking. The door of the truck opened and out stepped her brother! Minnie said in a very loud and happy voice, "Selvie! Selvie, is that you?" as she ran down the stairs towards the truck. The both of them stood there for a moment, and then they gave each other a big hug. Selvie looked up at the door of the house, and there standing in the doorway was a little girl. She looked at Selvie and pushed the door open. It was his daughter, Elise. Seeing her, Selvie was so full of joy, and his eyes were full of tears. Elise was four years old, and at this time, Minnie would have her at her house as if she were one of her own children. Elise looked at Selvie and called him daddy and put her hands in the air for him to pick her up. He smiled, this made him feel so good.

Selvie sat on the porch with his sister. They were talking catching up on things the both of them had missed out on over the years. Meanwhile, you could hear the sound of tires rolling over the dirt and rocks on the road, and you could see a very big truck that was fast approaching the house. The truck slowed down and then stopped at the side of the house. Selvie exclaimed, "It's our uncle Miles!"

Uncle Miles walked toward the both of them and yelled out, "Hey! I sent word by mail that we would be here soon." There were four others who had also come to visit., and now everyone was getting out of the truck.

Selvie walked over to his uncle and gave him a big hug. He said, "Man, I sure did miss you." He also asked his uncle where his wife was.

Uncle Miles answered, "Oh, she stayed back home in Chicago. My wife just can't take the heat, it's too much for her. I just brought some of my grandchildren." He was telling Minnie that his grandkids were the same age as her older children. Uncle Miles asked,"Where are Christine, Beatrice, Martha, and Robert? I want to give these kids a chance to get to know one another. We are family." He added, "Besides that, I miss being in Mississippi. You know this will always be my home. People don't realize that living in a big city is real different than living in the country."

Minnie called out to her older children: "Christine, Bee, Martha, I want you to meet your family." She explained to Miles that Robert would be there later on that day. All of Minnie's children came out onto the porch and into the yard, everyone except Christine, who was still out with Earl.

Uncle Miles said to the children, "Don't stand there looking at each other, introduce yourselves." They stood there for a moment, a little bashful, but then everyone started to laugh.

Minnie asked, "Where is Christine?" It was getting late in the evening. As soon as Minnie had asked, they could see Christine walking down the road toward the house. Christine had had her new friend Earl drop her at the end of the road, not wanting to explain who he was. Finally, she reached the yard where everyone was gathered. Minnie said, "If you want to continue to hang out with your friends, they need to drop you off at the door."

Christine said, "Yes, Momma."

"Now, come over here and meet your cousins," Minnie said. "This is Max, John, Sheila, and Joann."

One of Minnie's children spoke up and said, "Would you like to play on our swing that our dad made for us?" All the children said yes at the same time. McKinley had made them a swing out of an old tire and some strong rope that hung from a tree. Most of the children went to the back yard to chat and also toss a ball around. After awhile, McKinley arrived home. He was very excited to see everyone. So, just like his father used to do, he would entertain company by pulling his truck up to the side of the house and turning on the radio to one of the local radio stations. McKinley was letting everyone know they were going to celebrate that night. The children came running so very excited when they heard a very popular song. It was "Chattanooga Choo Choo." The children started to dance and sing. They were having the time of their life.

Not too far away, Mr. Roy Brintal was driving his truck down the dirt road. He had already passed by the road to the Newtons' house but couldn't resist when he heard the music and turned his truck around. He pulled up in the front yard, got out of his truck, and said, "Good evening." Everyone answered him back with "Good evening." Mr. Roy Brintal had been drinking. The spirit of the liquor had him feeling good. He said, "I like your family. I know that you are some good niggers." Mr. Brintal walked over to the side of the house. McKinley didn't like his behavior. He made it a point to keep his eyes on him to determine what his intentions were. Mr. Brintal watched the children dancing for a moment, saying, "Oh, yeah." Then, in a very loud and drunken voice, he said, "Now, which one of you want to dance with me, dance on my lap? I love the way you little colored girls move your bodies. I want you all to dance for me." Then he made a gesture, come here. Mr. Roy Brintal leaned back on McKinley's truck and started to open up his pants.

McKinley shouted in a very loud voice, "Okay, okay, it's time for everyone to go into the house."

The children, not knowing what was going on, started to complain, saying, "Aw, Dad, do we have to? We're having so much fun."

McKinley, not wanting things to get out of hand, repeated himself, but this time he was getting very angry. "Get in the house, I mean NOW!" Mr. Brintal found himself standing there looking a little foolish. With a stern look on his face, McKinley said, "You have a good day, sir." Mr. Brintal turned around and walked back to his truck. McKinley stood on his porch until Mr.

Brintal was gone and out of sight. He was not pleased with what had taken place, yet he was contemplating what might have happened. McKinley was very angry as he walked back and forth on his porch. He repeated to himself over and over, "I can't live here anymore."

Minnie heard him and said to her husband, "Where are we going to move to?" Uncle Miles and Selvie had watched everything that had taken place. The both of them tried to comfort McKinley with conversation. Uncle Miles said, "Son, you know there is a very big world out there. You don't have to stay in this town or this state. In the North, you can have your own land, your own house. You can work for a company and they will give you a paycheck."

McKinley said, "Really?"

Selvie said, "Yes, yes. It's real different, trust me."

McKinley said that sounded good, but he added, "We can't afford to just pack up and leave. You know you have to have a place to go to. It's not like it's just me. I have a wife and 10 children. I will always do my best in taking care of my family." The rest of the night was spent talking to his family as they sat on the porch. McKinley said to Uncle Miles, "You know, what if I hadn't been there? What would have happened? Mr. Roy Brintal would have had his way with one of my daughters. I would have tried to kill that man, he's just so evil. I'm so glad that you were here to witness how sick he is. This is why I have to go talk to Mr. Will Montgomery. Yes, I will be there to see him. Yes, I have a plan."

"That is great," Uncle Miles said. The two of them talked into the wee hours of the night. The house was full of children sleeping on pallets that they had made on the floor. Uncle Miles slept on the sofa. McKinley had a very hard time calming down, but he finally made his way to bed.

The next morning, the sky was slowly brightening in the east. Soon, people were starting to wake up on this beautiful, sunny day. It was a Monday. Most of the house was still asleep. It was Beatrice, Joann, and Sheila up in the kitchen cooking breakfast. You could smell the bacon all throughout the house. Also, homemade pancakes with maple syrup. One by one, people were waking up to the irresistible smell. You could also hear Joann and Sheila talking to their cousin Beatrice. Yes, telling her how wonderful the city of Chicago was, the girls clearly wanting Beatrice to come back to Chicago with them. "Wow, Bee, it's time for you to take your place in this world." Sheila and Joann were talking very loudly. Minnie could hear their chatter as she walked into the kitchen.

Minnie said, "What on earth is going on? I could hear you all having so much fun." As the girls started to chuckle, Minnie asked, "What is so funny?"

Sheila said to Beatrice, "Ask your mom, ask her now." Minnie had a look on her face that seemed to say, "Okay, what's going on?"

Beatrice looked at her mom and pulled a chair out from the table for her to sit down on. Beatrice said to her mom, "You know how much I love you, right?"

"Yes, sweetheart," Minnie answered her daughter.

"Well, Mom, I want to go to Chicago. I would like your blessing. You know that I can take care of myself. I can cook and clean. I'm also a very smart young lady." Bea went on and on.

Minnie was sitting there with a big smile on her face. "I'm so proud of the beautiful young lady you have become," Minnie said, "Yes, you can go. It's your time to shine. You will be 14 real soon." Beatrice was very excited. Minnie went on, "You still have to ask your dad."

Just then, McKinley walked into the kitchen and said, "Ask me what?" Then house got so quiet you could hear a pin drop. McKinley said, "What is it you need to ask me?"

Minnie said, "Go ahead, ask him."

Beatrice put her head down as she said, "Dad, I would like your permission to move to Chicago."

McKinley got real quiet. All of a sudden he became enraged, talking very loud, saying, "Hell, NO, you are not going anywhere. As a mater of fact, you are just too young."

Beatrice said, "I'm going to be 14 years old this year. You married my mom when she was 13 years old."

McKinley said, "I told you NO. Now that is what I meant."

Beatrice looked at her mother. Her eyes were so full of tears, as she ran to her bedroom to cry. Minnie looked at Sheila and Joann. "Could you please give us a few minutes?" The girls nodded as they finished up their meal. Minnie looked at her husband. "Now, you know you are wrong. I have never interfered with any of your decisions. But this is our daughter. It's time for her to live her life. I know that I have been sick. Bea has to do everything from the cooking to the cleaning, and making sure that everyone is dressed and ready for school. On Sunday she teaches a Bible School class. It's time for Bea to go off and live her life. She is our daughter, not our slave or housekeeper."

McKinley sat there with a puzzled look on his face. He started to mumble underneath his breath. Finally, he said, "Well, you're right. I will take care of this. It just won't be right now."

Minnie said, "Okay, take your time. I just want you to make it right." Minnie got up from the table to go talk to her daughter. She knocking at her door, walked in, and sat on the side of Beatrice's bed. Taking Bea by her hand, she asked, "How are you feeling?"

Beatrice looked at her mom and said, "It's not fair."

"Sweetheart, give him a minute. I think your dad was just overwhelmed with the news. I'm giving you my blessing to live your life. There is only one thing I need you to do. It's going to bother me."

"Yes, Mom, what is it?"

"I want you to know that I love you. I want you to know how much I'm going to miss you." Bea gave her mom the biggest hug.

Meanwhile, McKinley was doing some yard work and also working on his truck. Uncle Miles came over to where McKinley was working. The two of them were talking and laughing, enjoying their time together. Uncle Miles said, "You know, son, you know I don't like putting my nose in anyone's business, but you have to let your daughter go. Look at it another way. She may not even like it, living in Chicago. So then she will move back to Mississippi. On the other hand, this is God's will."

McKinley said, "I know. You're right. I will tell her later on. Tonight I will give her my blessing."

Uncle Miles said, "Good, that is the right thing to do."

Later on that day, everyone was over at Minnie and McKinley's house for dinner, including all of Minnie's brothers. Robert had finally come over to enjoy the big celebration. There was music from the radio. The children were dancing all around the yard with joy. Minnie was making ice cream in the ice cream machine. She would heat milk and sugar all together. Then she would combine this with the rest of the ingredients: eight egg yolks, whipped together until they became thick, using vanilla extract. She would chip away at the huge block of ice and feed it into the machine that churned until it formed into ice cream. The rest of the family put all their different dishes together (a potluck) for an awesome celebration. Uncle Miles and McKinley were still under the hood of McKinley's truck talking about what was needed to make the truck run more efficiently. On the other side of the yard, everything was ready for dinner as everyone gathered to eat their meal.

After an hour of eating and good conversations, McKinley stood up and said, "Please, please listen up." Minnie placed her finger over her mouth. McKinley continued, "I want everyone to hear this. Beatrice, please come up front." Beatrice put her head down to clean her mouth with a napkin, and then she made her way to where her father was standing. Beatrice was still unhappy from earlier that day when her father had told her that she couldn't go to Chicago. Now McKinley said to the family members, "I want you all to see this very beautiful young lady who happens to be my daughter. She is smart and very educated. I also want you to know that she will go far in life. So with that being said, I want to be the first to express my blessing for Beatrice. Beatrice will be leaving us and will soon move to Chicago." As Bea heard this for the first time from her father, she put her hand over her mouth. She was in shock for a moment. She turned to give her dad a real big hug, and then she made her way over to her mom to give her a hug. Now, one by one, everyone came up to Bea to congratulate her on the news. McKinley in a very loud voice, "Eat, drink, and enjoy yourselves."

The singing and dancing went on for the rest of the night. Robert had been sitting back, waiting until everyone was done wishing his sister well. Then he walked over to his sister and said, "Hey, sis."

"Hi, Bob!"

Robert said, "I just wanted you to know how happy I am for you. I know you will do well, I know it, sis." Beatrice and Robert moved to the porch to continue their conversation and spent the rest of the night reminiscing. Beatrice was very happy spending time with her brother.

Beatrice said to Robert, "Please stay the night with us. I know that you don't have to go to work tomorrow. I will ask Dad if he can give you a ride on his way into town on Wednesday. Dad says he needs to take care of some business. Besides, Uncle Miles will be leaving in a few days, hopefully by the end of the week, maybe by Thursday.

As they talked, Beatrice could tell that something was bothering Robert. Beatrice asked him what was wrong: "What's on your mind? I can tell that something's not right, what is it?"

"Well, when I was at work the other day, I saw Christine in a truck with that man from y'all church. I think his name is Earl. I'm not sure what is going on. I know that Mom and Dad don't know about her seeing him, either."

Beatrice said, "Well, time will tell it all. Bob, it's getting late. Let me give you some covers and a pillow and help you find a place to rest tonight."

A few days had gone by, and it was a bright and early Wednesday. McKinley was up and on his way to the bank. He needed to see Mr. Will Montgomery, and also he had to drop off his son at his job. McKinley pulled up to the gas station. Robert was about to exit his dad's truck when he looked at his dad and said, "Dad, you need to know that Christine is courting this young man named Earl."

McKinley had a surprised look on his face and said, "What do you mean?"   "Well, I just needed to let you know,"

Robert said. "Thanks, Dad, for the ride," he added as got out of the truck.

"You have yourself a good day, son."

"You as well."

McKinley drove off and made his way to the bank. He entered the building and waited to see Mr. Montgomery. The receptionist approached McKinley when he had been waiting well over 15 minutes and said, "Mr. Newton, Mr. Montgomery is ready to see you."

"Thank you," he replied. Mr. Montgomery walked toward McKinley and they extended their hands to each other for a very stern handshake. "How can I help you?" Mr. Montgomery asked in his happy voice. He ushered McKinley into his office. "Please have yourself a seat, McKinley. How is the family?"

"Well, Mr. Montgomery, that is one of the reasons why I'm here to see you. I need a bigger place for my family. We have outgrown the place where we live now. I was wondering if you may have any other property available for us. I mean for us to sharecrop on. I also need to get 50 dollars out of my account. My daughter is moving to Chicago. I don't have much, but I want her to have something."

"Well, McKinley, I'm glad that you came by. There is a property that's not too far from where you live. I think you might like it. We will work out some arrangements soon. I will have a contact written out by the end of the week or, better yet, next week this time. You can move in soon."

McKinley replied, "Thank you, sir. You are one of the most honest and fair men I know. Thank you once again." McKinley walked out the door whistling. He felt so full of joy, even though he wasn't happy about the news of his daughter sneaking around with someone he was unfamiliar with. McKinley drove home. Minnie was in the kitchen cooking, and he gave her a hug and a kiss. She said dinner would be ready soon. McKinley then shared with his wife all the events of the day, even the news about Christine. By the time he was finished talking, all the girls had come in to set the table so everyone could sit down and have a meal together before Beatrice left for Chicago the next day.

Plates were clinking and pots were being passed as everyone was sitting down to eat. McKinley started the conversation with, "So, Christine, who is this young man that you're sneaking around with?"

Christine was very quiet, speaking carefully. "Yes, I'm seeing Earl. Earl Lindsey, and I love him." It was real quiet now, no one said a word.

McKinley started to speak, "What do you mean? I want to meet him. He has no right seeing you if he can't have your parents' permission. I need to find out his intentions."

Minnie just looked and listened to it all. The children were all in shock except for McKinley Jr. (June). He said, "Yes, Dad, they have me for the lookout person while they go for their walks in the woods. Oh, and Dad, they tell me to let them know if anyone is coming. I really don't know what they're doing out in the woods."   McKinley Sr. looked at Christine and asked her, "Is this true?"

"No, no, Dad, it's not what you think."

"Then if it's not what I'm thinking, tell me what is going on. I will have you take me over to his house. I'm not liking this."

Christine was still trying to explain to her dad, "Earl is a member of our church. Dad, I will introduce you to him this Sunday."

McKinley looked at Minnie. "I'm not liking this. My girls are growing up on me too fast." McKinley took a moment to gather up his thoughts. "You know, I'm not going to deal with this tonight. I will tackle this in the morning. Christine, in the meantime, I forbid you to see this man. Do you understand me? I need to meet him and his family."

Christine said, "Yes, Dad, I will do what you ask of me." Everyone was finished eating, so they all pitched in on the cleanup of the kitchen, washing the dishes and putting everything back in its proper place.

As the family was relaxing and getting ready for bed, McKinley said that he had a lot on his mind. He wished Uncle Miles and his children good-night and went to bed. Minnie came to bed shortly after McKinley. McKinley put his arms around his wife as they both lay in bed. "Minnie, I'm not liking all of this changing. My girls are growing up so fast, I'm just worrying about them."

Minnie replied, "Yes, dear, we have to keep our faith that God will protect them from all evil.

"I hope so. I really do." Then both of them fell asleep.

The big day had arrived. Uncle Miles was going back to Chicago! Everyone was up and packed and ready. The time had come to say good-bye. It was very emotional for the entire family. Beatrice grabbed her bags and walked out the door and onto the porch. Her mom and dad were standing there, both of them trying to hold back their tears. Beatrice said, "Well, Mom, it's time for me to go." She gave her mom a real big hug. Then she looked at her dad and took him by the hand, giving him a girly handshake.

Her dad handed Beatrice an envelope. "Honey, it's not much, but it's a start. Please take care of yourself. Wow, I can't believe I said that. I know you will be alright. Please write and call us. I want to know that you're okay." Beatrice said good-bye to her parents and climbed in the truck. Uncle Miles and the others said their good-byes as well. McKinley and Minnie watched the truck disappear down the road. Minnie just stood there, not saying a word. McKinley took her by the hand and leaned in to kiss her on her cheek. He said, "Momma, she will be fine. Beatrice is a very fine young lady, and I know that she will go far in this world." Minnie just stood still as if she couldn't go on without Beatrice. McKinley didn't say anything more to his wife as she was very deep in her thoughts. After about 30 minutes, Minnie walked to the porch and sat down in her rocking chair.

In the meantime, Uncle Miles was headed to Chicago. This was Beatrice's first time leaving the state of Mississippi. She asked if it was possible to stop by the gas station to say good-bye to her brother. Uncle Miles said, "Yes, I want to say good-bye to him as well." As they approached the gas station, they could see Robert there doing his job. Uncle Miles pulled up to the gas pump. He said, "Son, please fill my truck up." Robert said okay and everyone got out of the truck to say good-bye to him.

Robert went over to his sister Beatrice, saying, "You know when I get to Chicago, you will be the first person I see." Robert reached into his pocket, pulled out a 20-dollar bill, and handed it to his sister. "Beatrice, this is all that I have as of now. I want you to know how much I love you. Please take care of yourself."

Beatrice and Robert hugged each other, and Beatrice said to her brother, "Please look after our mom." Robert promised that he would.

Uncle Miles said, "It's time to go."

Robert said, "I will come to see you as soon as I can, I promise. I love you." Everyone got back in the truck, and Uncle Miles drove off down the road. You could see Beatrice waving in the back window of the truck until it was gone in the sunshine of the day.

Later on that day, it was time for the Newton family to get the house in order so they could make the move into their new house. Mr. Roy Brintal was going to come over to pick up the keys. Sure enough, there he was pulling up in the yard. He got out of the truck and said, "McKinley! A new family is going to move in here immediately. You will be out of here by this weekend, right?"

"Yes, sir, those are my plans. What is the problem?"

"I just don't understand why you want to move. You know, you just can't please all of you niggers." Meanwhile, McKinley's son Junior (June) was sitting on the porch and overheard how this man was talking to his dad, and of course he didn't like it. There was a water barrel that sat on the porch. June took a leak in the barrel--yes, he urinated in the barrel! He knew that Mr. Roy Brintal would want a cool drink. After Mr. Roy Brintal walked around the house and the yard, he stopped back on the porch before leaving. June had a big smile on his face. Mr. Brintal yelled out, "Boy! Don't just stand there, go fetch me a drink."

June answered, "Yes, sir. I know you are really thirsty. I know you want a big cup of water," and he got a cup of water for Mr. Brintal. As Mr. Brintal was drinking the water, June's smile got bigger and bigger.

McKinley told June to check on the other children who were playing in the yard, yes, his little sisters. One of his sisters had always loved fancy things. Very creative, she had collected many pieces of glass from old soda bottles in all different colors. Yes, she would dream big, telling everyone those were her diamonds. The other children would make baby dolls out of potatoes, by wrapping a cloth over the middle part of the potatoes, and also creating people out of sticks. Yes, they used their imaginations.

Meanwhile, not liking Mr. Brintal's tone of voice with him, McKinley started to load up the truck to make the move into their new place. Minnie was inside and had started to pack, with the help of her older girls. Everyone was busy packing. Then they could hear a truck coming down the road. It was Selvie (Uncle Marley) who had gone to get Robert to help. The both of them got out out of the truck. Selvie said, "Hey, sis, how have you been?"

Minnie answered, "I'm fine, we just haven't had much of a chance to talk." Selvie said, "I know. So, what is going on with your daughter Christine? I mean, I hear that she is courting."

Minnie said, "Yes, we are going to meet her friend Earl at church maybe this Sunday."

Selvie was holding two bottles of soda in his hand. He took his keys out of his pocket to open up the bottles and handed one to his sister. It was so hot outside. He took a drink and said, "AH, AH! This really hits the spot."

Minnie said to him, "What's going on with you? I mean, you are trying to run two households. Now, when you don't bother to come home to Annie, then Annie comes here looking for you. So, my question is, how long do you think you can continue to do this? It doesn't look good, your daughter is seeing all of this. She is like my child, and I care about her well-being."

"Sis, I know, I also appreciate the fact that you care for Elise and you treat her like she is one of your children and you are letting her grow up with your girls. I'm not sure why me and her mother Annie couldn't make things work. We could never see eye to eye on much of anything." As they were sitting there, the hot sun was beating down on them both and they could hear a car approaching, the tires rolling over the rocks making cracking sounds. They could see dust kicking up. "Hey, Minnie, who is this coming down the road?" asked Selvie. You could hear the children playing and running around in the back yard.

The car pulled up at their house and a man stepped out. It was Mr. Will Montgomery. He was wearing a gray hat, a white shirt, and his suit was also gray. He walked toward Minnie and Selvie, took a few steps up on the porch, and removed his hat. He nodded and spoke to Minnie and Selvie. "Good evening. How is everyone today? I was wondering if McKinley was home."

Minnie answered, "No. No, sir, he is not."

Mr. Montgomery said to Minnie, "You don't have to say 'sir' to me. You can just call me by my name, that would be just fine with me." Minnie looked at Mr. Montgomery and smiled. Mr. Montgomery said to Minnie, "Well, I just wanted to go over a few things. Would you please be so kind as to let him know that I stopped by? Thank you, and have a good night."

Minnie replied, "I sure will." Minnie was with her brother for the rest of that day as they packed up one house and then unpacked at another house. They put everything in its proper place at the new house. The both of them worked hard until they were tired. Eventually, Selvie told his sister that he was ready to go home, he was done for the night. Minnie gathered up her children and put them to bed in their new house.

It was very fortunate that McKinley had moved his family into a much nicer place. The sad thing was that being a sharecropper in Mississippi wasn't much different than being a slave. It entailed the same amount of physical labor. No matter what you did or how hard you worked, you were always at a disadvantage. For instance, when the crops were being weighed in at 100 pounds, the sharecropper would only get credit for 50 pounds. Now, a slave worked for nothing, while a sharecropper only had the opportunity to get the bad crops and would really work for much more than a month of rent. As a sharecropper, you would be given tools, farm animals, fertilizer, and seeds, but you would be working to produce a crop for your landlord. You would be charged a high rate for using their equipment. The landlord would control everything and also determine the crops' profit.

Yes, the Mississippi Delta was the richest cotton farmland in the country. McKinley had worked for Mr. Roy Brintal at a disadvantage. Mr. Brintal would also use very unkind words. McKinley was very happy with his decision to work for Mr. Will Montgomery instead. Mr. Will Montgomery had always been considered fair and honest, and his work conditions were much better. He worked very hard to make sure his workers were treated fairly.

Over the next few years, a lot happened. Christine married her fiancé, yes, Earl Lindsey. He had asked her father for her hand in marriage. They were married in their church, Good Hope.

It was a warm summer day, Tuesday, June 6, 1944. Christine was visiting her parents' home. Her husband was at work. He had promised to return by dinnertime. McKinley was on his way home. As he was driving down the road, he noticed some beautiful flowers in front of someone's house. He was feeling good, so he stopped. He walked up to the door of the homeowner and asked if he could possibly pick a few of their flowers for his lovely wife. The kind man who answered the door said he could. McKinley picked three roses. They were so big and pretty, so red, the smell of love so sweet. Thanking the kind man as he climbed back into his truck, McKinley was feeling good, singing and getting into his music. He had almost arrived at his house, and already he could smell his dinner cooking--the sweet smell of smothered pork chops with gravy, crowder peas, and mashed potatoes.

McKinley walked into the house, holding the flowers behind his back. He stood in the doorway and looked into the kitchen. Then he walked into the kitchen and leaned over his wife's shoulder to kiss her on the cheek. Minnie turned toward her husband. She was glowing all over. McKinley pulled his wife close to him. He couldn't get too close, though, because Minnie was expecting her eleventh child. McKinley took the flowers out from behind his back and presented them to his lovely wife. Minnie was a little emotional, and her eyes filled with tears. McKinley asked her, "Are you all right?" She said yes she was, as she reached for a jar to put the flowers in. Minnie put the flowers on the table and thanked McKinley for them.

McKinley said, "You are so very welcome. Well, I'm hungry. I will wash my hands to get ready for dinner. I will go get the children ready for dinner as well." Their house didn't have running water. There was a well in the back yard. The children were very excited that their dad was home. They would ask him a million questions. McKinley got himself all cleaned up as he enjoyed entertaining the children, and they all went into the house and sat down at the table. McKinley looked over and saw his first child, Christine. He said, "Hey, I didn't even know you were here." McKinley couldn't help but notice that she was also pregnant. He was taken aback for a moment. He said, "Where is your husband?"

Christine answered, "He is at work. He should be coming to get me real soon."

"Okay, let us pray over this delicious food." Everyone bowed their heads as their dad led them in prayer. Shortly after McKinley was done praying, plates were made. Oh, the table was full of chatter, everyone wanting to get a turn to speak and tell their dad how their day had gone. McKinley had the radio on in the living room when they all heard the radio announcer repeating himself, "D-DAY, D-Day, I repeat, D-Day."

On June 6, 1944, more than 160,000 Allied troops landed along a 50-mile stretch of the north coast of France to fight Nazi Germany in World War II on the beaches of Normandy, France. "D-Day" was a code that was used for the invasion. On that day, there was an estimated casualty count of 4,000 to 9,000. There were 4,414 confirmed dead. McKinley couldn't help but think about how he could have been there fighting in the war. Although he was very saddened about the news, he was also very grateful for the blessing of being spared. So, on that day, McKinley took the time to reflect on God's grace and mercy. He ended the day with prayer and gratitude.

A month had gone by. It was now Independence Day. It was a day of celebration, and the families were getting together. Everyone would be gathering at McKinley and Minnie's house. One by one, Minnie's brothers came over with their families. All the children were growing up so fast. The picnic tables were ready. The men of the family were taking care of all of the food. A pig was being roasted on the open-pit grill, tied to a steel rod until it was fully cooked.

Minnie was moving a little slowly that day. Yes, she had help from her sister-in-laws. Dinner was almost ready; Minnie was unable to resist in helping to prepare the many side dishes. Minnie's son June came outside to tell her that his sister Christine wasn't feeling well--she was complaining that her stomach was hurting. Minnie was very concerned for her daughter and stood up to go into the house. She took a few steps, and a gush of water ran down her leg. The other ladies knew then that everyone was in for a long night. The children knew that they needed to go and get their dad and they ran yelling, "Dad! Dad! There's something wrong with Mom." McKinley rushed over to help his wife into the house, holding her up and guiding her to the bedroom. The sister-in-laws helped Minnie get undressed and gave her a bed bath.

About 30 minutes had passed, and Minnie knew that she would be giving birth to their child very soon.

Minnie was very concerned about her daughter who was in the next room. Christine was now being comforted by her husband. Yes, a lot was going on. McKinley went to get the local midwife. McKinley's mother was no longer delivering babies. Miz Martha was up in age and felt that she wasn't able to do that anymore. Everyone was trying to comfort both Minnie and Christine.

McKinley returned with the midwife. Her name was Miz Jean. The both of them entered the house. Miz Jean said, "Where is Miz Minnie?"

"I'm in here, Miz Jean," Minnie answered.

Miz Jean entered the bedroom and said, "Okay, let me see what is going on." Miz Jean asked everyone to leave the room so she could see how soon this baby would make its way into the world. Miz Jean checked out her patient, checking her cervix, and announced out loud, "This baby will be here in the next hour. I can feel the crown of its head." Miz Jean asked Minnie, "Are you in any pain?"

Minnie answered, "No, not really. I guess I'm more worried about my daughter Christine in the next room."

Miz Jean said, "Yes, I'm on my way in to check on Christine as we speak." Minnie said, "Okay, please keep me informed about my daughter."

Miz Jean said, "I will." She was in the room with Christine for about 20 minutes, giving her a full examination. When she went back into Minnie's room, Miz Jean could see that Minnie's pain had increased. Minnie asked how Christine was doing. Miz Jean said, "She is in early labor and has a ways to go. I believe maybe a baby by tomorrow. I'm more concerned about you. I'm going to check and see where you are at in your delivery."

Minnie yelled out, "I feel the baby coming out, this baby is ready."

Miz Jean said, "Let me check." She lifted the sheet up to look, and the baby's head was halfway out. Miz Jean yelled out, "It's time," as she grabbed for a clean towel to catch the baby. Miz Jean told Minnie, "Push." The baby was making its way out. Then Miz Jean said, "Oh, I have a healthy baby in my hands."

Minnie looked at Miz Jean and said, "Please don't tell me I have another baby girl."

Miz Jean said, "I won't tell you that. I will say to you, you have a new baby boy."

Minnie looked at Miz Jean and said, "Thank you." As Miz Jean slapped the baby on his bottom, he cried out loud.

Miz Jean went into the living room where everyone was sitting and informed McKinley, "Your wife has given birth to a baby boy."

McKinley was very excited as he went to his wife's side. He kissed his wife and then took his son into his arms. He kissed his son and said, "Thank you, God, for another healthy baby."

Miz Jean asked, "What will you name your son?"

McKinley looked at Minnie, and then he answered, "Well, we talked about this earlier. We have decided to name him after both of his grandfathers that he will never have a chance to meet. His name will be Walter Henry Newton." So, on July 4, 1944, a new baby was born.

Meanwhile, in the next room was their oldest child and her husband. The night was very hot; everyone was expecting a long night. Miz Jean stayed close by to make sure everything was all right. Miz Jean was in and out of Christine's bedroom, checking on her, putting cool towels on her forehead. Christine had started to fall asleep for a few minutes at a time. Yes, she was so exhausted from the pain of being in labor. Yes, her husband Earl was sitting next to her holding her hand and also telling his wife that everything would be all right. In the other room were her parents who couldn't help but worry about her. This being Earl and Christine's first child, Minnie couldn't help but reminisce on the day that she had given birth to her first baby, thinking about how her mother had been there when she needed her. Minnie got up the strength to walk to the next room and sit on a chair next to her daughter's bed. Minnie took Christine's hand, holding it to her heart, and with her other hand she brushed Christine's hair with her fingers. Christine looked at her mom, smiled, and said, "Why are you not in bed resting and healing? I hear that I have a new little brother."

"Yes, you do," Minnie replied. Minnie leaned over and gave Christine a kiss on her forehead and told her daughter, "I love you."

Christine said, "Mom, I love you too. I need you to get your rest, Mom." Minnie answered, "Yes, I will. I will come back soon. I just need a few hours of sleep." Minnie returned to her bed.

Miz Jean was in and out checking on Christine, and she noticed that her water had finally broken. It was approximately 3:00 AM on the morning of July 5, 1944. Christine's labor had increased. The pain was unbearable. She was having a very hard time giving birth to this child. Her husband had to leave the room for a brief moment. McKinley was in the living room to try to support his daughter and looked out the door and saw Earl sitting on the porch. He was in tears. McKinley asked him, "Son, are you going to be all right?

Earl answered, "Yes, sir. It's just that I had to get myself some air. I didn't want Christine to see me break down in front of her. I need to be strong for my wife." McKinley said, "Son, I understand. It's not easy seeing someone in pain like that."

The next moment Christine yelled out from her bed. Miz Jean ran to the room. She checked on Christine and then said, "It's time." Miz Jean had some clean towels and a basin of hot water by the foot of the bed. "Now Christine, I need you to push when I tell you to." Miz Jean held onto Christine's legs and told her to push. This went on for 20 minutes. "Okay, the baby's shoulders are out," and then in a very commanding voice, she said "Push!" The baby fell into the hands of Miz Jean who said, "Oh, we have another little boy. You have a son."

Christine asked, "Can I see him?"

Miz Jean said, "Let me clean him up first." She slapped the baby's bottom and he began to cry. All bundled up in a towel, Miz Jean laid the baby in Christine's arms, with her husband right by her side. "He is so handsome." Both Earl and Christine were kissing the baby on his cheeks. Christine was beaming with the joy of just having given birth to her son. Miz Jean had given them their special moment to bond. Now she returned to the room to wrap things up because her job was done. "Okay, you two, what are you going to name your baby?"

Earl hurried up and answered, "He will be named Earl Lindsey, Jr."

Christine said, "Yes, yes he will."

Miz Jean did some paperwork and handed them some important information on the clinic to take the babies to. She said, "My job is all done. I want to congratulate you all on these two beautiful babies." McKinley gave Miz Jean $20 for her work. She said, "Have yourself a wonderful day."

The day was busy; everyone came over to see the new babies. Minnie was very familiar with taking care of babies. She knew how vulnerable babies can be to germs, so she wouldn't let too many people hold her baby. Minnie was very worried about Christine doing too much too soon. Christine was talking about going back to her house the same day that she had given birth, and Christine and Earl gathered all their things up. Baby Earl was wrapped in a thin blanket. The weather was a very hot 95 degrees Fahrenheit.

Minnie and McKinley had talked to both Earl and Christine about how important it was for her to get her rest. Minnie was trying to give Christine some pointers on motherhood and shared with her some of the information her own mother had given her. Minnie said to Christine, "Let me hold my grandson." When Minnie picked Earl up, she noticed that he had a very runny nose, and she took a cold towel and cleaned his face. Minnie told Christine, "Please keep an eye on him. It could be something very serious. I really wish you would consider staying here a few more days. I know I can't tell you what to do anymore. I can only give you some good advice."

"Mom, now you know I can do this," said Christine. A few minutes later, Earl was helping his wife and their new baby into their truck. Minnie was watching them as she stood on the porch seeing them off. McKinley was in the bedroom, watching over their baby, Walter. Minnie walked back into the house, feeling exhausted and needing some rest. Over the next few days, Minnie and McKinley were loving on their children, and Minnie was getting the rest she needed so badly.

Now, over the next few days, Christine and her family were trying to bond. But something was off. Christine was worried about her son. It was that cough that he had. His little body just kept coughing and coughing. The cough had developed a peculiar sound. It went a little like this: "whoop-whoop-whoop," as if he couldn't catch his breath. Christine had expressed her concern to her husband. They were talking to each other and hoping and praying that the cough would stop. One very long night, when Earl Jr. was just a few days old, both parents were walking back and forth worried, trying to comfort their son. Finally seeing that things hadn't gotten any better, only taking a turn for the worse, Earl and Christine make a decision. They hurriedly gathered up a few things and got in the truck and sped down the road to the hospital. Then Christine, sitting in the passenger seat holding the baby in her arms, let out a big cry, "My baby, my baby is not breathing! Earl! Earl! He can't breathe! My baby is blue!" She was crying and yelling in a frantic state of mind. Earl decided to drive to the closest place he could, which was his in-laws' house. They made it to Christine's parents' house with Christine jumping out of the truck holding her baby in her arms, holding him close to her chest, and then running for the door, tripping up the stairs, yelling, "Mom! Dad! Please help! Please help me!"

Christine opened the door. All of the children that were in the house had gotten out of the way. It was as if they knew that something was terribly wrong. The little ones were peeking out the bedroom door. Minnie and McKinley had heard the cry for help and rushed out of their bedroom. As everyone met up in the kitchen, Christine laid her son on the ironing board. Minnie listened to what her daughter was saying and took her finger to sweep the inside of baby Earl's mouth to make sure he wasn't choking on something. Then, placing her mouth over his little mouth, she blew small puffs of air into his little body. Minnie continued doing this for about 15 minutes or more. Christine and Earl stood there watching, both crying. Earl took his arms and placed them around Christine, trying to comfort her, knowing that Earl's little body wasn't moving at all. Minnie looked at her daughter to tell her it was too late. Christine fell to the floor yelling, "No! No! My baby, my baby is okay."

Minnie and McKinley grieved for their daughter. They had to call the local funeral home to come and get baby Earl. Christine wouldn't get up off the floor. She held her son in her arms, rocking him and singing to him. She sat there for the next four hours before Minnie had to literally get down on the floor with Christine. She looked at her daughter and said, "Can I hold him?" as she reached out her arms. Minnie held the baby close to her heart. McKinley and Earl Sr. put their arms around Christine to give her comfort, and she put her head on her husband's chest and cried. He held Christine, telling her how sorry he was.

Then they all heard a knock at the door. McKinley answered the door. The man at the door explained that he was there to take the baby to the funeral home. He wanted to know if a doctor had seen him as they needed a death certificate before he would be able to take the baby with him. McKinley said in a very quiet voice, "Yes, the doctor is on his way, so if you don't mind, could you please wait here on the porch? He should be here shortly."

Now it took about an hour before the doctor arrived at Minnie and McKinley's house. The doctor was a white man who worked at the neighborhood clinic. He came in the house and sat at the kitchen table. He was wearing black slacks and black Stacy Adams shoes and a white shirt with a black tie. He was carrying a black doctor bag. He also had on some thick glasses. You could tell he needed them to see. He laid his glasses on the table, and a few minutes later he was fumbling for them even though they were in plain sight. Minnie was sitting on the couch still holding the baby. Christine was in her old bedroom with the other children with her husband right by her side. The doctor asked, "Where is the mother of the child?"

Minnie said, "She is in the other room."

He said to Minnie, "May I go and ask her a few questions?"

"Yes," Minnie answered.

The doctor knocked on the bedroom door and asked Christine, "Are you the mother of the child that has passed?"

Christine, standing in the bedroom, answered, "Yes," as she put her head down.

"I just need to know in your own words what happened." Christine then explained what had gone on. The doctor listened. When she was done, he said, "Thank you. Oh, I'm sorry I didn't tell you my name. I'm Dr. Scott DeVries. You can call me if you need to talk about what happened. I'm going to examine the baby so I can rule the cause of death." Dr. DeVries walked into the other room and reached out his arms to Minnie, who handed the baby to the doctor. The doctor was done with his examination in 30 minutes. The man from the funeral home was still there waiting. Dr. DeVries opened the door to make a gesture for the young man to come, and then he handed the baby to him with a death certificate. The doctor then said to Minnie and McKinley, "The cause of death is a disease called whooping cough." The doctor explained pertussis to them, better known as whooping cough.

After the doctor left, the house was real quiet; nobody knew what to say to each other. After awhile, McKinley called his family into the kitchen and started to speak. "I know that this is very hard for everyone. Yes, we will all get through this together." McKinley prayed over his family, asking everyone to bow their heads. When he was done praying, he said, "In Jesus' holy name, Amen." The rest of the night was spent loving each other. As for Christine, over the next few years, she spent all of her time getting an education

Two years had gone by. Now the year was 1946. The president of the United States of America was Harry S. Truman who led the U.S. in the final stages of World War II and also through the early years of what we all know as the Cold War.

President Truman was influential in the Democratic party. He was also known for advancing the cause of African-American civil rights. No president of the United States had supported civil rights before. Many people were very surprised at his involvement with the civil rights of Black Americans, considering the highly segregated environment in which he was raised in the state of Missouri.

McKinley was always very interested in the news on the radio as he listened to President Truman. He would sit there for hours listening. He loved to hear the support from the president of the United States, to hear him openly saying that all people should be treated equally, and that everyone had the right to an education at the same school as everyone else. It was so refreshing to hear this on the radio. Even though there civil rights laws had not been enacted yet, the president's thoughts and support were for Negroes—Black Americans. Often McKinley would call out to Minnie,"Oh, did you hear that?" Minnie would answer yes. McKinley was very much up on the news. He knew what was going on locally as well as nationally and internationally.

After listening to the radio for awhile one day, McKinley needed a break to eat the lunch his wife had prepared for him. As he made his way from the living room into the kitchen, he noticed the mail that was lying on a table and saw a letter addressed to him with a Chicago return address. The penmanship on the letter was impeccable. As McKinley proceeded to open the letter, he became extremely nervous and dropped the letter a few times. He calmed himself down by taking a few deep breaths. He knew that the letter was from the man he had heard about all his life. Yes, his father, Henry Nixon, not the man who raised him, but his blood father. The letter talked about some land that Henry owned in the cities of Edwards and Vicksburg, Mississippi. Henry Nixon wrote about how he wanted to help McKinley and his family with this land. McKinley was so excited about this news that he was jumping for joy all around the kitchen and grabbing Minnie in a loving way. He started to explain what the letter was about. Meanwhile, there was a knock at the door. It was Selvie. McKinley could see who it was from the kitchen. "Come on in," McKinley said.

Selvia asked, "Hey, what's going on?" He could tell that McKinley was in a very good mood. McKinley told Selvie his good news. Selvie said, "Wow, that is so wonderful." Then he added, "Well, since we are talking about good news, I have some good news as well."

McKinley said, "Okay, what is your good news? It's such a coincidence that you have received good news too."

"Stella has received a letter from this city in Michigan called Grand Rapids. There is this hotel. The name of the hotel is the Pantlind Hotel. They are in need of a head cook. So Stella and I and your son will be leaving soon for Grand Rapids."

"Wow," McKinley said, "that is great. I know that you all will do very big things. I hear that in the north you can own your home."

Selvie said, "Yes, you can."

McKinley said, "You told me that my son Robert is going with you?"

"Yes, he is."

McKinley said, "I know that I can't tell Robert what to do. I wasn't there for him as a father should be. Yet I still worry about him. I want what is best for my son. Tell me something, Selvie, do you think Robert would be in your way?"

Selvie said, "You know what? Let me tell you about your son. Robert is one of the most loyal and honest young men I know. Yes, let me add to that the fact that he had to raise himself. So, please give him your blessing."

McKinley held his head down and said, "Yes, I will send him off with my love and my blessing." Selvie looked at McKinley and smiled, giving him a thumbs-up signal as he walked outside to the porch where some of the older children were playing. Selvie laughed and joked around with them.

McKinley had had time to contemplate the information he had received that day from his biological father, Henry Nixon, and he was still feeling very happy about it. He also knew that it was time to talk to his own son Robert, so he drove to the gas station where he knew Robert would be diligently working at his job as a gas station attendant. McKinley parked his truck at the back of the store. He got out and walked over to where his son was working. Robert looked up and saw his dad standing there in front of him. Robert said, "Hi, Dad.

McKinley said, "Hi, son. I just had a talk with your uncle Marley."

"Dad, I knew that you would come to see me as soon as you heard the news."

"Well, hold on, son, it's not what you think! I came over here to give you my blessing. I know that you will do well. I came to find out how soon you will be leaving."

"Well, Dad, I believe by next week. I have a lot to do before I go north. I need to let Mr. Roy Brintal know that I'm leaving."

"Well, son, please let me tell him. In the meantime, keep this information to yourself. Son, there is this old saying, 'Don't let the left hand know what the right hand is doing.' I will tell him the day that you leave. I believe if you tell Mr. Brintal too soon, he will somehow try to sabotage your plans. Son, I'm happy for you." McKinley stood face to face with Robert and opened up his arms to give his son a big hug. The both of them were trying to hold back their tears. McKinley cut off his emotions by saying, "Oh, wow, I have to get back home to your momma. I'm sure she has some work for me to do."

Robert said, "Okay, Dad, I will talk to you later."

Over the next few days, Robert spent a lot of time at his parents' house, when he wasn't working. McKinley was trying to give his son the best advice that he could. "Son, I know that you can handle yourself when you need to. I know that you will do well. I just want you to know that the best thing you can do when you're around people you don't know is to not be too quick to speak. Always sit back and listen. A person will always show you who they are and what they are about. You have good common sense."

"Thanks, Dad. I really appreciate this conversation." Robert was on the sofa listening to his dad's advice. McKinley was distracted by one of his other children, and Robert's mind had started to wander and he started thinking about his mother who was in the kitchen washing the dishes. Robert stood up and walked to the kitchen door. "Hi, Mom, how have you been?" he asked.

Minnie said, "I'm doing very well. I was told you're moving north with your uncle and Stella.

"Yes, Mom, I'm going to miss you the most. I love you, but at the same time, I don't really know a lot about you. I just know you're my mom. I want you to know one thing, Mom: Trust me, I will come back to Mississippi for you and my brothers and sisters. I want better for you and for them. I know that there has to be a better life out there. Mom, I hear people talking at the gas station about how well the Negroes are treated in the north."

"Yes, son, I know how determined you are. I have no doubt that you will go on and do great things. I love you too, Robert. Now, I know that you're staying for dinner."

"Yes, ma'am, I'm staying." A few hours passed. It had gotten dark outside, and Robert was sitting on the porch of his parents' house. Robert loved music and had learned how to play the guitar on his own. He had taught himself the blues. That night was one to remember as Robert was able to experience what he had longed for all of his childhood: time with his family. He enjoyed his time with them long into the night. Yes, he even spent the night on the sofa. In the middle of the night, Minnie would get up and give all of her children a big kiss while they were sleeping. That night, she reached over to give Robert a kiss thinking he was asleep, only to find that he was still awake. He was finally able to fall asleep with a huge smile on his face.

A week had gone by. It was time for the big journey to the north to Grand Rapids, Michigan. Selvie and Stella were all packed up and on their way to pick up Robert at the gas station. Robert was ready, and he was very excited. Minnie and McKinley were at the gas station to see their son off. McKinley helped Robert put his things in the back of his uncle's truck, and then it was time to say their good-byes. McKinley said, "Well, son, we can never say good-bye. How about we say, I will see you later?" Robert hugged his dad and then his mom.

Selvie said, "We'd better go now because we have a very long ride ahead of us. We will have to stop for rest along the way."

Selvie, Stella, and Robert climbed in the truck, and Minnie said, "Wait, I prepared you a good meal. It's not always safe to stop. Not everyone is friendly. I also didn't want you to be hungry." She handed Robert a large bag.

"Thank you, Mom."

McKinley asked, "Which way are you going to travel?"

Selvie answered, "I will be going north on Route 45. It will take us into Chicago. Then we plan on finding our way from there to Michigan. I need you to stay tuned to the phone. I will try to call you. I want you to know when we arrive."

"I will do just that," said McKinley, and he and Minnie stood there as they drove away. McKinley looked over at Minnie and said, "Where has the time gone? My son has become a man."

Now, after being on the road a few hours, Selvie, Stella, and Robert were listening to the radio enjoying some of the latest R&B and blues singers. "Voo-it! Voo-it" was one song. Then there was Bull Moose Jackson, "I Know who Threw the Whiskey Bottle (in the Well)." Let's not forget the group called The Ink Spot. I could go on and on. There wasn't any secret about Robert's love of music. It gave him comfort, it was soothing to his soul. Robert turned to his uncle and said, "Please tell me about Grand Rapids Michigan."

Selvie said, "Son, I know it has to be better than where we come from."

"I really hope so."

Selvie took his time on the highway, and he was careful of his surroundings. Stella had also prepared food for them so they wouldn't have to stop at any diners along the way. As for being a Negro in the year 1946, you couldn't just walk into any diner and expect to be served. More than likely, you would end up dead or in jail for no apparent reason. So when traveling, it was just the wisest thing to have your own food. When Selvie had driven for over 10 hours, he decided it was time for a rest. They had made it to the other side of Chicago, still in the state of Illinois, not close to Grand Rapids, Michigan. They still had a ways to go. So they found a spot to pull off the road. It had gotten dark, so they made a small fire with some branches that were lying on the ground. His truck was parked close to the little campfire. The back gate of the truck was down, and Stella was sitting on it. Selvie and Robert were sitting on a big rock nearby. Selvie rolled himself up a cigarette and started blowing smoke out of his mouth, looking at his nephew who was deep into his thoughts. "You asked me about Grand Rapids? I will tell you what I know. I know that there is so much as far as opportunity in that town. Trust me, we will be okay. I'm not going to keep us up tonight talking because we need our rest and we need to be on the road as soon as possible."

"You're right," Robert and Stella agreed. They all lay down to sleep, and when four hours had gone by, Selvie woke up and was ready to go. He wanted to drive as far as he could. He also knew that he was close to his destination.

The Pantlind Hotel in Grand Rapids, Michigan, was the reason Stella left the south and moved to Michigan. She was offered a position as one of the head cooks at the hotel. The hotel was known far and wide for its hospitality as well as its exquisite cuisine. It was considered one of the top 10 finest hotels in the United States in the year 1946. Its original owner was J. Boyd Pantlind. The address was 187 Monroe Avenue. Not too far from this hotel is the Grand River, which flows from one end of the city to the other. The Grand River runs from Hilldsale County in southeastern Michigan all the way west to Grand Rapids, Michigan, and finally ends in Lake Michigan. A road runs alongside the river, and many people would travel on this road. It was kind of like a guide to let you know where you were as far as traveling from the east to the west in Michigan. This road is called Grand River Avenue.

      After the long drive to Michigan, Selvie finally drove into the city of Grand Rapids, known as Furniture City because it was a center where furniture was manufactured that was sold all over the world. The city was breathtaking. It was a very different place than what they were used to—it was larger and less restrictive. They could feel the difference. But one thing that was very apparent was that the city was segregated. Negro people were separated from others and were not really allowed to live anywhere else but on the southwest side of town. Division Avenue was the street that ran north and south and divided the city from the east to the west.   Stella had contacted friends in Grand Rapids before moving there, making sure that they could stay with them until they found a place of their own to live. It took them about a month to find a place for the three of them. They rented two rooms from an old friend named Hester Sumrall. Mr. Sumrall would help anyone in need. About a week after they arrived in Grand Rapids after they were situated with their friends, Robert and Selvie started to gather information about job opportunities. There were so many places to go to apply for employment, and so many people wanting to work.

      Gypsum Mines, a company that manufactured plaster, was founded in 1898. This place stood out because it was said that the pay was good. Also, it was said they were hiring people every day. One of the gypsum mines was located one hundred feet under the bed of the Grand River, with the mine shaft located at the most westerly span of the Blue Bridge over the Grand River, formerly the Grand Rapids and Indiana Railroad Bridge. The founder of the company was its owner, William T. Powers. Selvie and Robert went to apply for a position at Gypsum Mines. The two of them had only been in town for a week and were hired immediately. They were so excited.

Both Robert and Selvie worked countless hours down in the mine, making sure they earned enough money to pay the rent and also saving some. About a month after they started working, they called to Mississippi to share the good news about their success. It was a Sunday afternoon. Stella was cooking a wonderful dinner of pot roast, sweet baby carrots with green beans, white diced potatoes, cornbread, and tall glasses of iced tea. While they were waiting to eat, Selvie said, "Okay, it's time to call your dad. We haven't talked to him since we came here. We won't talk too long because it is a long-distance call."

The phone rang in Mississippi, and McKinley answered, "Hello."

"Hey there, this is your brother-in-law Selvie. I just wanted to check in on the family."

McKinley said, "Well, everything is fine. We have a new baby born on March 19th." Yes, the year is 1946.

Selvie said, "Wow, I didn't see that one coming."

McKinley said "It's just one more mouth to feed. He is a healthy baby boy. We named him Cleotha Newton."

"Well, brother-in-law, congratulations."

McKinley said, "Thank you. I want to know, how are you all doing? Tell us what it's like in Grand Rapids. I hear it's a fabulous place. Maybe I will come to visit when I go to Chicago to see my dad, Henry Nixon. I want to go see Bea as well." McKinley talked on and on, not letting Selvie put Robert on the phone to share the good news about his new job.

Selvie finally said to McKinley over the phone, "Hey, your son wants to talk to you."

McKinley said "Oh? Okay, put him on." Selvie handed Robert the phone.   "Hello, Dad. I'm sorry we haven't called you before now. How is Mom doing? I will be home to visit soon. I'm working very hard for a brighter future. Dad, did I hear you say I have another little brother?"

McKinley said, "Well, son, yes, you do."

"I'm sorry, Dad, we are going to have to talk another time. This call is long distance."

McKinley said to his son, "Okay, we can talk maybe next week."

Robert said, "Okay, that would be nice." Robert hung up the phone, and then he sat down on a chair in the kitchen. His uncle was standing close by.

Selvie looked at Robert and asked, "What's the matter with you? Are you all right?"

Robert answered him, "Well, no, I'm not. I'm worried about my mom. I'm worried about our family. I know how much they are struggling. I just want better for my family. I would love for them to move here. This place is nice compared to where they live now."

Selvie said, "You're right, son. I'm trying to work very hard so I can have my own car."

Robert said to his uncle, "Me too. Now in the meantime, let's eat this wonderful dinner." The both of them sat down with Stella and enjoyed their meal together.

Over the next six months, Robert worked very hard and saved all of his money. It was a sunny Saturday morning, and Robert was so excited. Robert had waited for this day to come, because it was the day he was going to buy himself a new car. He asked his uncle go with him. Selvie had ridden around town looking at car dealerships. First they went to the Pontiac dealer on Madison Avenue, but they were not happy with what they were looking at. Next, they went to the Ford dealership. As soon as Robert got out of his uncle's truck, he spotted his car. "Wow," he said to his uncle, "there it is. That is what I want." It was a Super Deluxe Tudor Sedan, a BRAND NEW CAR! The sticker price was $1,125.

Selvie said, "Well, that's a lot of money. Do you have enough?"

Robert answered, "Yes, I have saved up $1,500."

Selvie said to his nephew, "Let me do the talking."

The dealer made his way over to them and said, "May I help you?"

Selvie answered, "Yes, I'm interested in buying a car."

The dealer wasn't sure if he was for real or not. He said, "Well, that would cost a tremendous amount of money."

Selvie was chewing on a toothpick in the side of his mouth. He answered the man, "Yes, we are very much aware of what it would take to purchase a car. My question to you, young man, is, are you interested in making a sale? We are interested in buying the car that you have on display, the Super Deluxe Tudor Sedan."

The dealer said, "Okay, let me get this car written up for you. I will have you come into my office." He seated them in his office, walked out, and left them sitting there for approximately 30 minutes. The dealer finally returned and said to them, "With the taxes and bill of sale, the total amount is $1,200." Selvie placed $1,200 on his desk in cash. The dealer said, "May I ask where you work?"

Selvie was still chewing on that toothpick. Then he answered real slowly, "Gypsum Mines--does it really matter? As long as we have the money, that should be all you need to know."

The dealer said, "Here is the paperwork that you will need for ownership."

Selvie said, "I don't see the title."

"You will receive that by mail real soon. Here are the keys to your new car, Robert," he said, as he handed the keys to Robert.

Robert took the keys with this a smile on his face and said, "WOW, this feels good." Over the next few weeks, as he drove his own car back and forth to work, he thought about his big accomplishment.

Robert had some time off work coming up soon. He wanted to take a trip down to Mississippi to let everyone know how life was in the north. He also wanted to try to convince his father to move to Grand Rapids, Michigan. Even though his dad had not looked out for him when he was growing up, Robert was thinking about his family. He especially wanted the best for his mother who now had a total of 12 children, with nine of them still living under their roof. Robert was the kind of person who always believed in people and wanted to make things better for them.

It was time, and Robert had made it to Mississippi. He took his time and made it there in two days, only because he drove there alone and needed time to rest along the way. Now, Robert was standing on the porch of his parents' house. He knocked on the door. His dad answered, and McKinley was very excited to see his son. In a very loud voice, he said, "OH. WOW! Minnie, it's Robert. Hurry! Hurry! Come see our son." It had been a year since they had seen him. Robert had grown so tall. McKinley looked at his son and said to him, "You are a man now." After a few minutes, the whole family was on the porch, hugging and kissing Robert and telling him how much they missed him.

No one paid any attention to Robert's new car until McKinley asked, "Did someone let you use their car to come down here for a visit?"

Robert replied, "No, Dad, that is my car."

McKinley said, "Really?"

"Yes, Dad, it's my car. I have worked so very hard to be able to buy the things that I want."

McKinley was so proud of his son, and he showed him by praising him for his labor. "Son, come on in and tell me about this place you call home."

The both of them sat down at the kitchen table. Minnie said, "I will make you both some breakfast."

Robert said to his dad, "Well, the people, I mean the Negro people, look out for one another. Yes, they are good people. On Sundays after church in the summer months, people go out to Johnson Park to have a picnic and share their meals. They are all listening to good music, playing baseball. Then you can drive your car on the back road of the park. They call it the Snake Road. Yes, I must say it's fun. Monday through Friday, I'm working over 40 hours a week. Dad, then you get this paper check. That is what they call it. You take it to the bank, and then they give you cash."

"Well, son, I know about the bank."

"I mean, Dad, I make about 95 cents an hour. I work all the overtime I can. I bring home $100 a week."

"That's not too shabby," McKinley said. "And you don't have to give anyone any of your money?"

"NO, Dad, NO! It's your money, all of it."

McKinley said, "Wow!"

Robert started to eat the meal that his mom had prepared for him. He enjoyed each and every morsel of it. After he had finished, Robert asked if he could lie down and take a nap. Minnie said, "Yes, you don't have to ask."

Robert was so tired that he slept until the next day. He woke up to the smell of his mom cooking again. Minnie was in the kitchen making dinner for the family. Robert walked over to the table in the kitchen, pulled out a chair and asked where his dad was. "He is out in the yard doing whatever it is that he gets into."

"Mom, how have you been?" Robert asked.

"I'm fine, son."

"Mom, I wish you and Dad would come to the north. It's really nice, and I believe you wold love it. They have toilets on the inside of the houses with running water, and it smells a lot better than these outhouses." Minnie just looked at Robert and said that would be nice. It was a little before noon, and Robert was enjoying his talk with his mom, the both of them laughing.

McKinley walked in the front door and asked, "What is so funny?"

Robert said, "Oh, nothing, Dad."

"I'm glad you are here, son. Hey, let's go down to where you used to work. I want Mr. Brintal to see that you are a man now, a successful man. Son, I'm so proud of you." Robert and McKinley jumped into Robert's car and drove to the gas station where Robert had worked as a young child. On the way to the station, Robert talked about all that he had seen on his way to Grand Rapids. The both of them were able to laugh. Now they were at the station. They had to pull up to the gas pump that the Negroes had to use. Robert and his dad got out of the car.

Inside the store, Mr. Roy Brintal could see them standing by the car. Mr. Roy Brintal walked outside and over to where they were standing. He said, "Where did you get this car? I believe you must have stolen it. It has out-of-state3 license plates on it."

McKinley said, "Oh, NO, SIR. No, sir. No such thing."

Mr. Roy Brintal looked at Robert and said, "BOY, I didn't like how you just walked away and quit your job and had your dad tell me later that you had moved on."

Robert said, "Well, yes, that's about how it happened. You were told that I would no longer be working for you anymore. Am I right?"

"Wait a cotton-picking minute. Whose car is this?" McKinley looked at his son, hoping that he wouldn't answer. But Robert was so proud; he said, "Well, that is my car."

Mr. Roy Brintal said, "You mean you work for a white man that lets you go put gas in his car? Ain't that right, BOY?" Robert stood there without a fear in his heart or in his bones. Mr. Roy Brintal said, "You address me with 'YES, SIR.' You must have forgotten where you came from."

Then Robert spoke very loudly and very clearly: "Let me tell you something, Mr. Roy Brintal. Where I live, we don't have to address the white man with 'YES, SIR' or 'NO, SIR.'"

Mr. Roy Brintal had this weird look on his face and told them to get off of his property and, "NO, you won't use my gas. Oh, McKinley, you should teach your BOY the consequences that will come his way! Don't be surprised if you find your BOY hanging from a tree, okay?"

"YES, SIR, we are leaving," McKinley said, "Come on, son, let's get out of here. Give me your car keys." In a very frantic manner, Robert drove quickly back to the house. Then McKinley said to Robert, "Give me your car keys. You stay here until I make it back." Robert handed his keys to McKinley and waited for him on the porch, trying to understand what had happened, thinking that by leaving the ways of the south, he should be treated with respect. After being gone for about 20 minutes, McKinley returned with fear in his eyes as he walked towards his son. He could hardly talk, he was so afraid. He said, "Son, get your things. They will be coming for you. Lord knows what they may try to do. I don't want to take a chance on anything happening to you. I would never forgive myself for doing nothing. Son, drive and don't stop for nothing, not even to use the bathroom. Don't stop until you're out of the state of Mississippi. You have enough gas to make it to the state of Tennessee. Once you reach there, you can stop in Chattanooga to gas up your car. Now, remember, son, not everyone is your friend."

Robert told his dad, "I will be back soon, real soon."

McKinley said, "OKAY! OKAY! GO! GO! GO NOW!" Robert got his things, walked over to his car, got inside, and drove off. After four hours had gone by, McKinley was wondering how far Robert had gotten up the road, hoping and praying that he had made it out of the state of Mississippi, also knowing that Mr. Roy Brintal would be up to something.

McKinley gathered up all of his children, making sure they were all accounted for, and told them to remain in the house until it was safe to go outside. They were all together in the same room, and McKinley held onto his Bible and started to pray. Just as he was finishing his prayer, they all heard a loud noise. A rock had crashed through the front door, and they heard the glass shatter and fall to the floor. They also heard dogs barking outside in front of the house. The children cried out of fear, not understanding what was going on. McKinley told everyone to get down on the floor. He also told Minnie, "I have to go out there and try to talk my way out of this mess." McKinley grabbed his wife and gave her a very passionate kiss. He told her how much he loved her. Then he let go of her hand and dropped to the ground and slid along the floor on his stomach. It took him a minute to make it to the door. Then, in a very loud voice, McKinley said, "Mr. Roy Brintal, Robert isn't here." His voice was trembling as he said, "Please, sir! Leave us be, please."

McKinley slowly opened the door and stood up very slowly. He could see about ten men standing in his yard. Some had dogs and some had torches. Mr. Roy Brintal yelled out, "Where is he?" He has to be taught a lesson. Where is he?"

"I don't know, SIR!" I have no idea where he could be." McKinley was standing there, shaking in his boots. Then one of the men with a dog let the dog loose. It happened so fast--the dog leaped up on the porch, barking and growling, and charged for McKinley. The dog opened his mouth and grabbed hold of McKinley's leg and wouldn't let him go. McKinley yelled out. The dog was strong, and McKinley had to lie on top of him to stop him from doing him any more harm. Only when the dog's owner called for his dog to stop did he stop attacking McKinley. One of the men yelled out loud, "NEXT TIME IT WILL BE WORSE. TELL YOUR SON THIS IS FAR FROM OVER. I CAN'T HAVE ANY OF YOUR PEOPLE THINK THAT I'M WEAK."

McKinley said, "YES, SIR," not wanting them to harm anyone else. He knew that Robert would be safe because he had made a good start back to Michigan. Mr. Roy Brintal called off his posse and they went their way.

McKinley went back inside the house. His wife had heard everything. Now her concern was taking care of her husband's medical needs. McKinley had a very bad wound on his leg. Minnie had him lie down. Then she started a fire in the wood-burning stove so she could boil some water to clean his leg. His pants were stuck to his leg, all intertwined with skin and blood, but Minnie was able to get her husband all cleaned up and dress his wound. McKinley was left feeling exhausted as well as humiliated. It didn't feel good to be treated like that in front of his children. But one thing McKinley was happy about was that none of his children were harmed.

Robert had made his way to Illinois, and then he arrived in Chicago. He had not seen his sister Beatrice for some time now, and he missed her very much. Beatrice was now married and thinking about starting her own family. Robert wanted to see her, and he also needed to rest. He stopped to get gas. He wasn't sure he would be able to find Beatrice. Robert found her number in his wallet, and he was able to reach her by phone. She was so excited to hear from her brother. Beatrice gave Robert step-by-step instructions to their home. Robert finally arrived at the address his sister had led him to. He wasn't sure he had the right place, but he got out of his car and walked toward the door. He knocked four times, but no one answered, so he started to walk away. Then, when his back was toward the door, the door finally opened. He heard a sweet little voice saying, "Robert?" He turned around, and there was his sister Beatrice. She was excited to see him and said, "Wow, you have really grown," as she gave him a big hug. "Come on in," she said. "I know you must be hungry."

"Yes, I am," Robert said.

"I wish you could meet my husband, but unfortunately he is at work. But he should be home soon." Beatrice fixed Robert a plate--fried fish, cole slaw and deep-fried hush puppies. A tall cold glass of iced tea.

Robert told Beatrice, "Man, that really hit the spot. I am so full." He thanked her for the wonderful dinner. Robert and Beatrice talked for hours before Robert asked if he could lie down. He was extremely tired and needed to rest. He wanted to get up early and be on his way back to Michigan. Beatrice showed him where he could rest for the night. She told him good-night and closed the door, and he went fast to sleep.

Early the next morning, Robert got up thinking he would be on his way without disturbing anyone in the house. But, to his surprise, when he walked into the kitchen, he saw that Beatrice was up and had made breakfast. She had already seen her husband off to work. Robert repeatedly thanked Beatrice for her hospitality. Beatrice told him, "You are my brother and I love you dearly." As she continued to talk, she pulled out some envelopes, all addressed to her. There were 12 of them. "I want you to take these envelopes with you. If for any reason you need me, or if you are in any kind of trouble, I want you to put a letter in the mailbox, and then I will know to come help you. In the meantime, I'm going to try to get Mom and Dad to move here to Chicago, or maybe to Michigan. I talked with Mom and Dad, and I'm not liking what is going on. Also, Robert, please give me a phone number where I can reach you."

Robert said, "I will give you the number where I stay. The number is Cherry-5-7053."

Beatrice said, "Thank you."

"Okay, sis, I need to get on the road. It's time for me to go. I don't want the day to get away from me.

Beatrice said, "Okay, Robert, you take your time making it back to Michigan." She waved to him as he got into his car, seeing him off on his trip.

Now back to work, staying very busy, Robert kept to himself. One afternoon after a very hard day at work, one of his co-workers noticed how quiet Robert was and walked up to him and asked him what his name was.

Robert said, "My name is Robert."

The co-worker said, "My name is John." John asked Robert, "What do you do for fun?"

Robert answered, "Well, not much. I love my music. I play the guitar, I love the blues."

John said, "Oh! I know a place where you can hear the blues. Hey! Maybe you would like to go shoot a game of pool? You know, maybe one day after work. How about on the weekend?"

Robert said, "Yes, that would be very nice." So, from that point on, John and Robert were very close friends. One day in the lunchroom at work, there was a very big conversation among their co-workers about the re-election of Harry S. Truman. It seemed like no one could talk about anything else. Robert entered the lunchroom, and John wasn't too far behind. Both of them sat at the break-room table, listening to the other men talk, minding their own business. John changed up the conversation and started talking about how his truck wouldn't start, telling Robert how he had promised to take two of his church friends to get some stockings after work. He was wondering if he could get a ride home from work that day.

Robert told John, "I can give you a ride home from work, and I can also give you and your friends a ride to the store."

John said, "That is great. I will call and let them know that we will be by their house later on today. They don't live too far from here. They live on Butterworth Street."

Robert said, "Okay, no problem." Later on, when they were finished with work, Robert and John clocked out for the day. John got in Robert's car with Robert and gave him directions on how to get to his church friends' house as Robert drove. "We are here," John said when they arrived at his friends' house. "Let me go to the door to get them. You know, their mom raised two ladies, and I need to show nothing but respect." Robert sat waiting in the car, not sure what was going on. After a few minutes, he could see John standing on the porch opening up the door as two beautiful young ladies walked outside.

Robert acted fast and got out of his car so he could properly introduce himself to the young ladies. Right away, Robert was very smitten with one of them and said, "Hi, my name is Robert," as he took off his hat.

She said "Hi," with a smile that could light up a room. "My name is Katherine, and this is my sister, Althea."

Robert was speechless just for a moment, but he managed to walk Katherine to the car and open the door to the front passenger seat. John and Althea sat in the back seat of the car. Robert took his place in the driver's seat and asked the women, "Where would you like to go?"

Katherine answered, "What about the drugstore on Wealthy Street?" Robert drove them to the drugstore, and Robert asked if he could go inside with Katherine. She said, "Yes, that would be fine."

At the checkout, Katherine was going to pay for a few things when Robert said, "Oh, let me pay for that, please."

Katherine smiled and then said, "Thank you." Before they left the store, Robert asked her if she like to have a milkshake with him. Katherine smiled and said, "Yes, I would. Thank you for your kindness. Thank you for taking me and my sister to the store on such short notice."

Robert said, "Oh no, I'm so very happy to do so." Robert seated Katherine at a table in the section of the store that had ice cream and milkshakes. As Robert went to the counter to order, John and Althea sat down nearby. Robert and Katherine talked for a few hours. Then Katherine said that she and her sister needed to get home. Robert said, "Yes, by all means. The time has gotten away from us. I really enjoyed talking with you. Um . . . let me ask you something."

Katherine said, I'm listening."

"Well, I know you don't know me yet. Well, I was wondering if you would consider going out to dinner with me."

Katherine hesitated for a moment and then answered him. "Yes, I would like to go out to dinner with you." Robert was elated as he escorted Katherine back to his car, and then made sure to get her and her sister home safely. He parked his car outside of their house and then hurried to the passenger side of his car to open the door for Katherine, holding her hand as she exited the car. He walked her to the front door and asked if he could have a kiss. Katherine said, "NO! I don't kiss on the first date, and this isn't even our first date."

Robert smiled and said, "Yes, you are absolutely right. You deserve the best, and I will show you the best that life has to offer."

Katherine smiled and said, "I will see you soon." Katherine and her sister went in the house and closed the door behind them.

Robert and John walked back to the car. The both of them talked for a few minutes before leaving. Robert said, "Wow, I have never felt this way before, man. She gave me butterflies in my stomach. Is this what they call love at first sight? I can't stop thinking about her. Wow! Me just thinking about Katherine makes my heart skip a beat."

John said to Robert, "Is this what God says about Order My Steps? All that I can say to you is, Congratulations. I know the two of you have not officially gone out on a real date, but I see nothing but the best for the both of you."

Robert proceeded to take John home. When he dropped him off, he said, "Thank you."

John said, "For what?"

"I want to thank you for introducing me to my wife."

"Your wife?"

Robert said, "Yes, I'm going to marry her. You'll see."

The next year was 1948, and over the next two years Robert dated and then married his beautiful wife, Katherine. In the year 1950, Katherine and Robert had their first child. Katherine gave birth to a baby girl, and they named her Gloria Newton. Robert was so happy that he couldn't dream of being any happier. Robert would go to work for his family, making sure that he provided anything and everything he could. Katherine and Robert purchased a new house that they could call a home. A home full of love and joy. The both of them would attend church.   Yet, Robert couldn't help reminiscing about his family in Mississippi. Robert remembered his childhood and how his dad hadn't been a father to him. Yes, he remembered how many times he wished his father would just take him fishing or even to church. Robert kept thinking about his mom, and he knew that the only way to make her life better was to make his dad's life better. Not to mention his younger brothers and sisters. Robert always believed in helping others and helping them to better themselves. Robert had found out through his job that Gypsum would be hiring soon. He was thinking about his younger brother, McKinley, Jr. He also talked with his uncle Selvie. His uncle wanted to bring his daughter, Elise, to Grand Rapids, Michigan, to live permanently. So Robert had a conversation with his wife and told her that he wanted her to see where it was that he had come from. He had some time coming up for vacation. One day after work, Robert talked to Katherine and explained to her that the following week they would be going to Mississippi. Katherine told her husband that would be fine.

Approximately one week later, Robert and Katherine were making the long trip to Mississippi. They had left baby Gloria in Grand Rapids with Katherine's mother. As Katherine could tell right away, the south was different than Michigan. The people in the south would tell you how they felt and showed their prejudice. When they arrived at Minnie and McKinley's house, as Robert was parking his car, his dad came from the back yard to greet them. McKinley was really excited to see his son. Minnie was in the house and could hear all of the ruckus. She opened up the door and stood on the porch with a big smile on her face. McKinley asked, "Son, aren't you going to introduce us to your lady friend?"

Robert was getting the bags out of the car, and he looked up to say, "Dad, this is my wife; my wife, Katherine." To Katherine he said, "Katherine, this is my mom, Minnie and my dad, McKinley."

Katherine looked up with a pretty smile and said, "Hi, Mom and Dad. I'm so very pleased to meet you both." McKinley right away gave Katherine a big hug. Then Katherine walked up the stairs and gave her mother-in-law a big hug.

Minnie told Katherine, Come on in and make herself at home. I was in the kitchen preparing dinner for later on." Katherine asked if she could help her with the preparation for dinner. Minnie said, "No, you just keep me company."

"Yes, I would like that." Minnie and Katherine talked and laughed, and Katherine listened very closely to the stories that Minnie told. Katherine had shared the fact that she and Robert were married and also that they had had a baby not too long ago. Katherine showed her pictures of their baby.

Minnie was so excited. She said out loud, "I am a grandma!"

A few hours later, Minnie called everyone to dinner. McKinley and Minnie now had 12 children. Four of them were all grown up, and eight of them were still at home. Everyone came from all over the house and were present for dinner. Robert had to introduce each and every one to his new wife. Katherine smiled with joy as she met them all. McKinley asked everyone to listen up as he started to pray over his children and the food that was prepared for his family. Then McKinley said, "Okay, let's dig in." There was plenty of food, and you could tell it was good because in no time it was all gone. Then everyone pitched in to help clean the kitchen. As they were cleaning, the singing started and made the task so much more enjoyable. It wasn't long before the entire family had moved outside to the porch. The younger children were playing in the front yard. As the day slowly turned into night, one by one, they started to get tired and said their good nights.

Now the only two that were left on the porch were McKinley and Robert. McKinley had a knife and a big piece of wood and started to whittle away at it. He had his glasses on, and they hung down on his nose. He began to speak. "So, son, tell me all about this city called Grand Rapids, Michigan."

Robert began to tell his dad about the pros and cons of this city. "Dad, it has to be better than living in Mississippi. Dad, let me ask you something. Do you have dreams? Dreams of living in a better place?"

McKinley cleared his throat, and then began to speak very slowly and carefully. "Son, I'm not sure if you know this or not. My father, his name is Henry Nixon."

"Dad, I thought your dad was Frank Newton."

"Yes, Frank Newton raised me. He is the man who adopted me. Now, don't get me wrong. I love Frank Newton. He is the only father I know. I thank him and my mother for their love. If it wasn't for Frank and Martha Newton, I would probably be dead. You see, son, my birth mother was named Loula Hood. Loula was a young lady who attended Alcorn University where Henry Nixon was a professor. He had an affair with Loula. After a few months, Loula became pregnant with the professor's child. Loula was scared and didn't know what to do. She was running scared and married a young man named Jonathan. He loved her so very much. I heard he was a very good man. When Loula found out she was pregnant with her first child, yes, she knew that it was the professor's baby. The bad thing was Henry Nixon was married.   When Loula went into labor with the baby, she and her best friend Olivia took a train from Laurel, Mississippi, to Vicksburg, Mississippi. Through a relative of her friend Olivia, Loula met Martha Newton, and they stayed the weekend with the family. Loula wanted to cover up the fact that she had given birth to a son. Loula wanted to throw the baby in the river. But Martha Newton was able to change her mind. Miz Martha explained to Loula that she and her husband were unable to have children and it would be an honor for them to have the baby. Loula then gave her baby to the Newtons. Then she returned back home to her husband, Jonathan, and told him she had suffered a miscarriage. So, it was told to me. Loula and her husband, Jonathan, had a child the very next year. After that child was born, Loula was pregnant a third time and was not sure if it was her husband's child or not. Loula then lost her life giving birth to that baby that was breech.

"Now, son, what was it that you wanted to say?"

"Well, Dad, June and Elise are moving to Grand Rapids, Michigan. We will be going back in a few days. Dad, I want you and mom to move as well."

McKinley took a few deep breaths. Then he said, "YES! YES, I'm ready, I'm ready to move. I just need to tidy up some things."

Robert let out a sigh of relief. "Dad, tell me something. Why did you tell me this story about Loula and Henry now?"

"I know that I haven't been the best father, and I'm not making any excuses. I never got the chance to meet my birth dad. I never understood why he couldn't find it in his heart to meet me."

Robert looked at his dad and said, "Why? Why couldn't a father be a father to his son?" Robert rubbed his head with tremendous thought. A few minutes had gone by. "Well, Dad, I'm getting very tired, and I'm going to go lie down and get myself some rest. Good night, Dad."

"Okay, son, good night.

It was about a year later, the year was 1952. Robert was able to move his entire family to Grand Rapids, Michigan, to humble new beginnings.

.

www.ingramcontent.com/pod-product-compliance
Lightning Source LLC
Chambersburg PA
CBHW071746120626
46550CB00002B/677